Yet even these bones from insult to protect

Some frail memorial still erected nigh,

With uncouth rhymes and shapeless scripture decked,

Implores the passing tribute of a sigh.

Their name, their years, spelt by the unlettered Muse,

The place of fame and elegy supply:

And many a holy text around she strews,

That teach the rustic moralist to die.

— Thomas Gray, ***Elegy Written in
a Country Churchyard,*** c. 1742-50

FRAIL MEMORIALS:
THE CEMETERIES OF LANGLEY

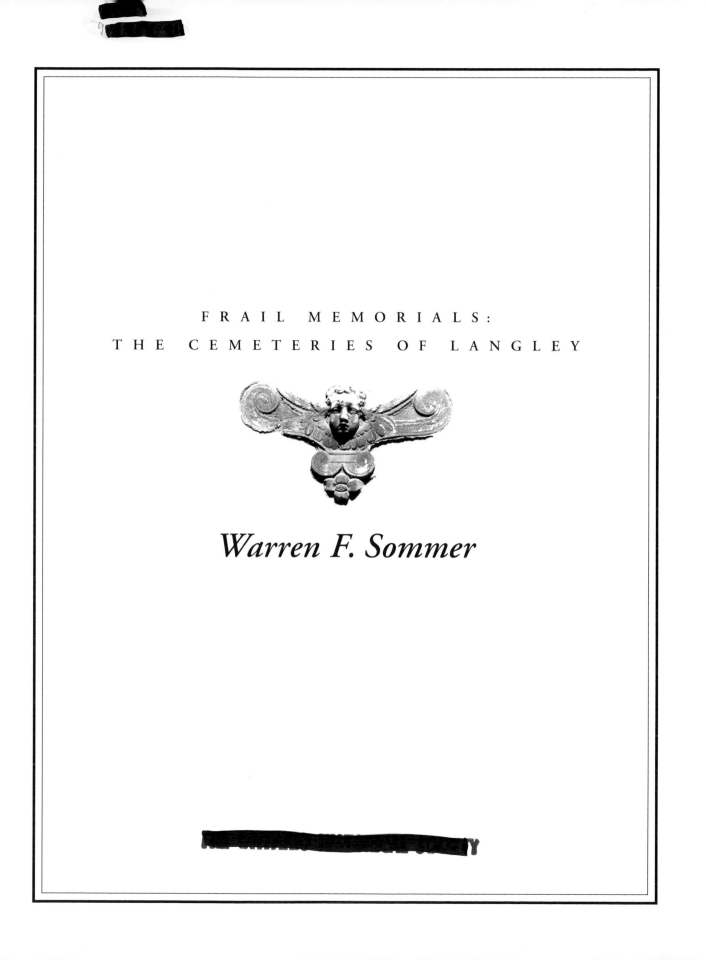

Warren F. Sommer

Library and Archives Canada Cataloguing in Publication

Sommer, Warren F. (Warren Frederick), 1951-
    Frail memorials: the cemeteries of Langley

    Includes bibliographical references and index.
    ISBN 0-9682654-1-3

    1. Cemeteries—British Columbia—Langley (District Municipality). 2. Langley (B.C. : District Municipality)—History. I. Langley (B.C. : District Municipality). II. Title.

FC3845.L35Z54 2005   971.1'33   C98-900631-X

Published by

Langley Centennial Museum & National Exhibition Centre
Corporation of the Township of Langley
9135 King Street (Box 800)
Fort Langley, B.C.
Canada V1M 2S2
www.langleymuseum.org

Inclusion of a cemetery within this document does not indicate that it is open to the public. If you are viewing these historic sites, please respect the privacy of owners and do not trespass on private property. Please do not take rubbings of any tombstone, as this can cause irreparable damage.

Readers with an interest in learning more about the history of Langley and the people buried in its cemeteries are directed to the online resources of the Langley Centennial Museum (www.langleymuseum.org). This website includes plot maps for the Township's cemeteries and records of over 8,000 Langley burials.

Cover painting by Brian Croft (*Walworth Cemetery – 1888*)

✿ *Contents* ✿

Foreword

CEMETERY and gravestone studies developed in North America as respectable and legitimate fields only in the second half of the twentieth century. Previous to that, antiquarian and genealogical societies had paid some attention to old cemeteries, but few others had. That changed in the 1960s when archaeologist James Deetz published articles about the distribution and use of symbolism in New England graveyards. After that, scholars increasingly began to see tombstones as documents that can help explain the past and to regard cemeteries as reflections of the societies during which they were in use. The founding of the Association for Gravestone Studies in 1977 acted as a catalyst for many individuals and organizations to find out more about the physical manifestations of death that surround us, but which we often overlook. From New England the study of tombstones, tombstone makers, and cemeteries has spread across the continent. Conferences, journals, books, and websites now abound about these topics, when only a few decades ago they were largely ignored.

In the 1970s, when cemetery studies were in their infancy, Warren Sommer and Mary Philpot were graduate students at the University of British Columbia. They began to talk about and document the province's heritage cemeteries. At the time, classmates and friends likely thought their interest was macabre, if not downright bizarre. Such was the attitude about cemetery studies only a generation ago, when death, dying, and the disposal of the dead were subjects that had become taboo in many places, certainly in Canada. Mary's thesis was a seminal work and paved the way for others who have studied and written about cemeteries in western Canada. Warren has maintained a continuing interest in the subject and has inspired many individuals, including me, to look at burial places in a new light. Over the years his research, writing,

and tours have proven to appreciative audiences that cemeteries are important places, worthy of study and preservation.

Frail Memorials has been a long time in preparation and could not be timelier. Though the importance of heritage has now been recognized in our society for many years, cemeteries are still often overlooked and neglected. Such neglect is especially ironic in Langley, which has more than a dozen cemeteries, including the oldest ones in southern British Columbia. The community's museums, archives, historic sites, and heritage buildings play an important role in reflecting our past, but what about the graves of those whose artifacts, papers, and houses are so carefully preserved? Poet Thomas Gray referred to his eighteenth-century English churchyard as "this neglected spot," but the same term applies to some of today's cemeteries in Langley and elsewhere. Warren's book shows categorically that cemeteries should neither be neglected nor forgotten.

The title of the book may surprise people who think that grave markers are almost indestructible. Because many tombstones are made of stone, this is a logical assumption. However, materials such as sandstone and marble – both used extensively for markers in nineteenth-century British Columbia – are prone to natural degradation. So is concrete, which was used to make markers, ledgers, or enclosures on many Fraser Valley plots. Even less durable were the large number of old graves that were identified by wooden boards, crosses, or fences that long ago succumbed to the ravages of wind, rain, sun, and grass fires. Even memorials made of cast or wrought iron are prone to rust and breakage. Zinc monuments, sold under the confusing brand name of "White Bronze," are found in one Langley cemetery. Although they are not subject to rust, they are susceptible to cracking and slumping.

Though nature plays havoc with cemetery markers, too often the greatest damage to them is caused by the careless, unthinking, or deliberate actions of humans. Sadly, Langley's cemeteries are just as prone as those in other places throughout British Columbia to the damage inflicted by vandals. Cemetery managers, too – whether churches, local governments, or independent organizations – have too often been guilty of inflicting irreparable harm to individual graves or entire burial sites while attempting to "clean up" neglected places or, worse, to simplify maintenance.

To a casual observer, all cemeteries may appear the same. However, funerary and burial customs vary widely from culture to culture and over time. British Columbia's existing cemeteries were developed after Napoleon's reforms of the early 1800s had been adopted in Britain and the United States. In the first half of the nineteenth century, Langley's modern cemeteries started as traditional Native burial sites. With each successive incursion of new arrivals – fur traders, missionaries, gold miners, and settlers – burial practices and cemeteries evolved. Langley's cemeteries clearly show these changes, and *Frail Memorials* provides an excellent primer outlining the broader context of trends in cemetery design and how they manifested themselves in one part of the Fraser Valley.

Cemeteries are like textbooks that document our changing communities and our changing attitudes to life and death. If you know how to "read" them, you have a useful key to understanding something about people and events from the past. Tombstone styles have gone through many changes: the wooden poles and boxes of ancient aboriginal burials; the simple wooden or stone markers of pioneer settlements; the elaborate obelisks and tablets of the late Victorian era; the small, impersonal plaques that were common after World War I; and, most recently, sandblasted stones that include portraits, pictures, and symbols that reveal something about the personalities and values of the people whose graves they adorn. The placement and layout of cemeteries also

explain much about how death was seen by people over time. Stó:lō burial sites were often situated in special places, such as islands in the Fraser River; the Hudson's Bay Company's burials were close to the fort; churchyards developed beside the earliest Christian places of worship where parishioners would walk past them on a regular basis; the first municipal cemeteries were laid out near, or close to, the centres of communities; and the lawn cemeteries of the twentieth century were created as far away from town centres as possible. Such changes mirror evolving trends in religion, politics, economics, and lifestyles.

Genealogy is one of the most popular leisure pursuits in North America. It can be frustrating for researchers to search in vain for tombstones that may never have been erected at all, or were cleared away by zealous cemetery managers in the mid-1900s, or were vandalized by unthinking louts. A book such as *Frail Memorials* is a wonderful benefit to anyone documenting a family in Langley. It provides a concise history of each burial site and useful references to some of the most outstanding monuments and well-known families at each location. Most importantly, however, it interprets Langley's long and diverse history in a new way for everyone, whether or not they have ancestors buried in the cemeteries described in the book. It is an asset to genealogists and historians alike and puts Langley in the vanguard of cemetery studies in British Columbia.

Researching and analyzing almost two centuries of information about Langley's cemeteries is a daunting challenge. Warren Sommer has triumphed, and his work will set the benchmark for other cemetery and local history scholars that follow. I hope it will also encourage a greater appreciation for heritage cemeteries wherever they are located and lead to increased vigilance to protect them.

John Adams
Founding President,
Old Cemeteries Society of Victoria

Acknowledgements

THIS book could not have been undertaken without the support of many friends and colleagues. The volume was conceived in 1997 during a conversation with Langley Township's former deputy municipal clerk, Kory Swaele, and Sue Morhun, the Township's manager of community and heritage services. This discussion resulted in a commitment to undertake a research project focusing on the township's burial places, with the ultimate intent of publishing the findings. I hope the resulting book will increase public interest and pride in the community's many cemeteries, several of which are among the oldest burial grounds in the province.

Some of the community's cemeteries – there are more than a dozen of them – are relatively well known, but several only came to light during the course of my research. I am grateful to Fred Pepin of the Langley Heritage Society for steering me toward some of the smaller cemeteries in the southern part of the township and to Penny Sogaard and her father, Dave Lockerby, for assisting me in my research on both the Walworth Cemetery and the 200th Street Burial. Bob and Sheila Puls, assisted by the late Alf Trattle, provided a number of leads regarding the cemeteries in the Derby townsite. Bob and Sheila's research into the burials in the Hudson's Bay Company Cemetery in Fort Langley has been formidable and deserves a volume of its own.

During the course of my research, Patty Catlin, Bryan Klassen, and Lisa Codd cheerfully provided access to materials in the archival collections of the Langley Centennial Museum, and Jacqueline O'Donnell was equally helpful with Langley-related materials in the City of Surrey Archives. Bill Lindahl answered a number of questions relating to current cemetery operations. Jerry Kotanko, a member of the Township's parks maintenance staff, provided access to information on individual graves,

and staff in the clerk's department supplied me with copies of the Township's old cemetery bylaws.

Phil Lawrence and Darren Seifred assisted me in my visits to the two small cemeteries on their properties. The late Bill Poppy helped me locate the approximate site of Ann McQuilken's lonely burial in south Langley. Bill and his wife, Helen, provided insights into the community's early funeral practices. Historian Norman Sherritt put up with an endless barrage of questions relating to the community's history. Yoko Goold kindly visited the Murrayville graves of two Japanese Canadians to translate the markings on their stones. Bill Marr provided considerable information about the cenotaphs and veterans' sections in the Fort Langley and Murrayville cemeteries.

As the manuscript neared completion, members of the Langley Centennial Museum's History Committee kindly agreed to review it. Their comments and corrections have been incorporated in the book. Michael Kluckner, Fred and Maureen Pepin, and Bob and Sheila Puls also reviewed the manuscript and caught a number of previously undetected errors. Bob Andrews generously produced a very fine map in very short order. Elspeth Richmond and Susan Murray undertook the production of the index within a very tight timeframe and have produced a very useful adjunct to the volume. Editor Naomi Pauls reviewed the manuscript just before it went to the designers. Working with Naomi was a delight and an education in itself. Her command of the English language is formidable and her insights have greatly improved the publication.

The highly attractive look of the book is largely due to the skills and creativity of four individuals. Artist Brian Croft kindly volunteered to create a painting for the cover, which illustrates the burial of members of the Walworth family in 1888. This is the second time Brian has provided a painting for one of my publications. I continue to be grateful for his generosity and artistic vision. Led by Craig Davies, the team at Design One Graphics Group has done a remarkable job of designing the volume. Designers Vanessa René and Terry Gherman undertook the detailed work on the project and have produced a very pleasing publication.

Although the book was only recently undertaken, its roots run deep. My interest in historic cemeteries grew in intensity during my years as a graduate student at the University of British Columbia in the mid-1970s. There, I was fortunate to meet Mary Philpot, who ultimately wrote her master's thesis on the subject of British Columbia's older cemeteries. Mary's enthusiasm for historic cemeteries was contagious, and her work complemented my own research into the province's historic churches, many of which sit amid the graves of former parishioners.

My friend and colleague John Adams, founder of the Old Cemeteries Society of Victoria, has been no less inspirational. I first met John at what was then called Heritage Village Museum in Burnaby and have enjoyed many conversations, slide presentations, and cemetery tours with him since that time. His contribution of a foreword to this volume is much appreciated.

Finally, I am eternally grateful to my wife, Bev, who has tramped through cemeteries with me on many occasions – and on several continents – during what were supposed to be vacations but which often became the subject of talks and slide presentations. This volume would not have been possible without her continuing patience and support.

Introduction

THE Township of Langley is a mixed urban-rural municipality of 303 square kilometres located in the central Fraser Valley. The Township is one of British Columbia's two oldest municipalities, incorporated at the same time as the Township of Chilliwhack, in 1873. The community's heritage is central to its identity. There are four museums within its bounds, and heritage-related celebrations such as Douglas Day, Fur Brigade Days, and Fort Langley's May Day are well-attended annual events.

The township has extensive heritage resources, a number of which are protected through legislation and other protective means. Heritage buildings such as the Fort Langley Community Hall, the Annand/Rowlatt House (in Campbell Valley Regional Park), and the Traveller's Hotel (at Murrayville's Five Corners) are central to the township's identity.

But one of the township's most important heritage resources has received little attention until now. Its cemeteries, the earliest of which dates from 1830, are among the most interesting and significant sites in the township. This study discusses a dozen or so such places, ranging from the isolated graves of little-known individuals to veritable cities of the dead.

Historic cemeteries offer glimpses into the lives and relationships of those who lived in our communities in both the distant and the recent past. Benjamin Franklin clearly understood the informational power of cemeteries when he commented, "To know the character of a community, I need only visit its cemeteries." For us, as for Franklin, cemeteries have the power to tell us who married whom, who begat whom, and where they were born. They speak of the horrors of epidemics, war, and of the far too frequent tragedy of infant and child mortality (seven of the first eight deaths recorded in Aldergrove were of children aged seven and younger). They evoke past hopes and beliefs, and recall the comfort provided by an abiding faith.

Cemeteries also reflect our own attitudes toward death. The cemeteries of the 1800s were intended as places for learning and contemplation. Today's cemeteries sometimes appear to be little more than crass disposal grounds, and their operators all too frequently seem more concerned with maximizing burial spaces and minimizing maintenance costs than serving social needs. According to a study undertaken by the Funeral and Memorial Information Council and the Wirthin Group in 1995, 29 percent of Americans associate cemeteries with sadness and death, while another 29 percent feel a sense of peace and beauty within them. There are those who are passionate defenders of cemeteries and those who feel they should not exist.

This publication aims to provide the reader with information on the history of cemetery design, monument making, and funeral services as they relate to Langley; to outline the history of individual cemeteries; to identify graves of interest in each; and to suggest how cemeteries can be interpreted as valuable social documents. Some of the monuments discussed are those of well-known Langley residents, while others have been chosen at random, where the words and designs on the stones seem particularly revealing. In the case of the Fort Langley and Murrayville cemeteries, the monuments discussed are generally arranged by date, with the oldest ones being listed first. In Fort Langley, the oldest graves are located close to the cemetery's Glover Road frontage, while the oldest graves in the Murrayville Cemetery are located in its northwest section.

FRAIL MEMORIALS:
THE CEMETERIES OF LANGLEY

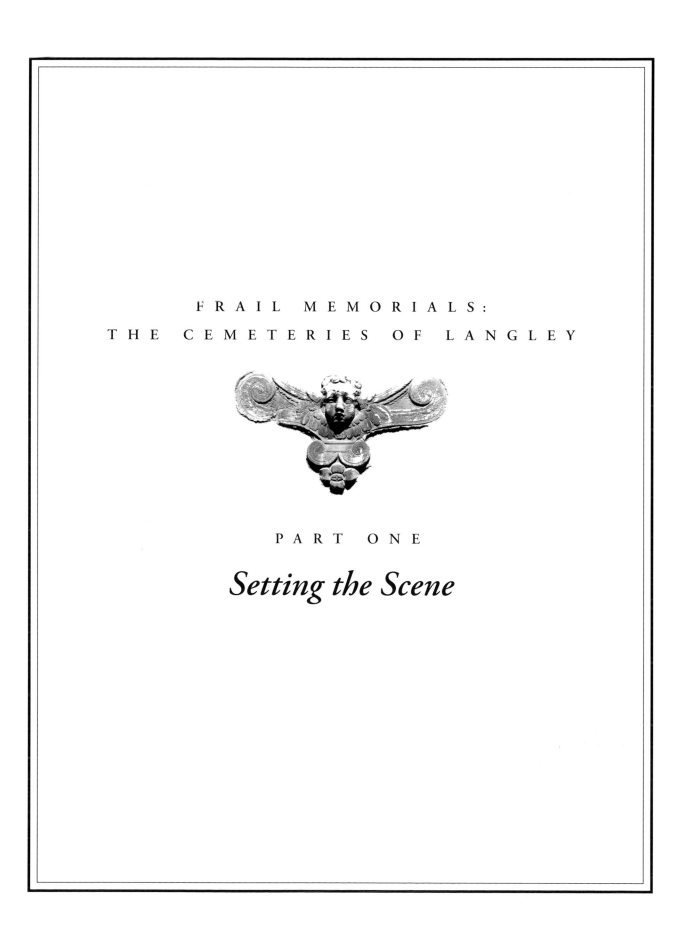

PART ONE

Setting the Scene

Langley: The Historical Context

IT is perhaps ironic that although the Langley area was among the first areas of the Lower Mainland to be explored by Europeans and the first to be settled by them, written records relating to the First Nations people encountered at the time of contact and early settlement are scarce. Most of our knowledge of the Native people who inhabited the area in the early nineteenth century is drawn from the *Fort Langley Journals* (surviving volumes date from the period 1827 to 1830), from the Hudson's Bay Company and federal censuses, and from anthropologists working in the field in the first half of the twentieth century. Although a few archaeological sites have been pinpointed in the north Langley area, little detailed exploration and still less excavation has been carried out.

THE STÓ:LŌ PEOPLE

Although there is no direct evidence to prove it, First Nations activity in the Langley area may date back as far as 10,000 years before the present. Sites in the Lower Fraser Valley, such as the Milliken and Glenrose Cannery sites have been dated to 8,000 to 10,000 years ago, to shortly after the last Ice Age. Archaeological evidence drawn from several sites suggests that Native people living in the Lower Fraser Valley became less nomadic – establishing large winter villages while periodically travelling to harvest natural resources elsewhere – about 5,000 years ago.

First Nations cultures were based on the wealth of the river and the forest. Salmon, sturgeon, and other fish were plentiful. These, and wild berries and tubers, formed the basis of the Native diet. The western red cedar was a source of timber for housing, canoes, household implements, and ceremonial items. Its roots were processed and woven into baskets, and its bark was transformed into clothing. The game of the forests and wetlands was an additional source of food, the pelts and hides being used for clothing.

In historic times, Native people are known to have lived in several villages in the Fort Langley area and to have utilized much of the adjoining territory for hunting, fishing, and gathering; as well as for spiritual quests. All these people are thought to have been Stó:lō, which in the Halq'eméylem language means "river." In the nineteenth century, at least, most were probably either Katzie or Kwantlen, two subgroups of the Stó:lō people. Prior to contact with European diseases, which appear to have spread to the south coast of British Columbia several decades before direct contact with European explorers, the Stó:lō population was much higher than it is almost two and one-half centuries later. Some authorities have speculated that before contact with European diseases, the Stó:lō numbered in the tens or scores of thousands, many more than the few thousand reported in the 2001 federal census enumeration.

NATIVE VILLAGES ALONG THE RIVER

By the early nineteenth century, the Kwantlen were the pre-eminent First Nations people in the Lower Fraser Valley, occupying villages in or having authority over much of what are today the municipalities of Langley, Maple Ridge, Abbotsford, Surrey, Delta, and New Westminster. When first encountered by Europeans in the early nineteenth century, the Kwantlen apparently had two significant villages near what later became New Westminster, as well as villages nearer the site of Fort Langley. The village of Skwekwte'xwqen stood at the site of New Westminster, while the village of Qiqa':yt (a fishing camp) lay opposite (on the south bank, in what is now Surrey).

With the establishment of the first Fort Langley in 1827 (at the site of the commemorative cairn in Derby Reach Regional Park), the main body of Kwantlen people are thought to have established a new village (Ts'elexwá:yel) near the mouth of Kanaka Creek, in what is now Maple Ridge. This was apparently done to secure a monopoly in trade with the fort and to derive protection from raiding parties travelling from elsewhere. When the first fort was abandoned and re-established at its current site in 1839, the Kwantlen relocated to McMillan Island. There, many inter-married with the fort's employees. Because of this, they became known to many as the "Langley tribe," while their reserve (allotted in 1879), became known as the "Langley Reserve." The Kwantlen, however, knew this site as Sqwàlets, meaning "the river went through." Although they now appear to be a

View of Kwantlen Village from the Third Fort Langley

single island, at the time the reserve was allotted, McMillan Island and Brae Island were separated by a slough. Interviews recently conducted with local elders of the Kwantlen First Nation indicate that the latter island was used in historic times as an area in which to fish and hunt. The island was also an area where berries, reeds, rushes, wild grasses, and other plant materials were collected for food, medical, and other uses.

Early anthropologists also referred to other Stó:lō villages near Bedford Channel. These include Snákwaya (the village of the "Derby people" who were extinct by 1824, at the mouth of Yorkson Creek), Slálomet (near the site of the first Fort Langley), Skwélic (a village of the Snokomish or Derby people on the west side of the Salmon River, at its mouth, which was wiped out by the smallpox epidemics of the late eighteenth century), and Husam (a village on the west side of the Salmon River, slightly to the west of its confluence with the Fraser).

There were also Katzie villages in the area. In historic times, the Katzie appear to have controlled Pitt River and Pitt Lake and had some presence near the mouth of the Pitt River, along the Fraser River. While their main reserve today lies on the north bank of the Fraser River, the Katzie also possess a smaller reserve (on the south bank, near the mouth of Yorkson Creek). Sources suggest that in the early nineteenth century, at least, the Katzie were recognized as the owners of significant sources of "Indian potatoes" (*wapato*).

It is difficult to determine which villages were occupied at the time of European settlement. According to Simon Pierre (1881-1967), anthropologist Diamond Jenness's main informant, the Derby people were extinct by the time the first

3

Fort Langley was established, and their two villages were abandoned. A British Admiralty chart of 1859, with corrections to 1865, shows a Katzie village at the mouth of Yorkson Creek. An American chart of 1869 confirms this information. As noted above, this small village continues to be inhabited.

The first written account of European contact with the area's original inhabitants dates from 1808, when explorer Simon Fraser, an employee of the Montreal-based North West Company, travelled down the river that was later to bear his name. Fraser recorded seeing a large Native village with cedar plank longhouses on the riverbank near what later became Fort Langley.

Langley appears to have been a permanent home for the Stó:lō as well as a crossroad and seasonal gathering place for other speakers of the Coast Salish languages. Natives from Puget Sound, Boundary Bay, and southern Vancouver Island are recorded by nineteenth century diarists as having used the Nicomekl and Salmon rivers (which were somewhat navigable in the 1800s) as a shortcut to the salmon fishery in the Lower Fraser Canyon. Seasonal visitors likely gathered in the West Langley area to harvest wild cranberries as well as to gather fish from the Salmon River near Fort Langley.

Records from the Hudson's Bay Company and others indicate considerable travel and trading by other First Nations people in the early to mid-nineteenth century. Prior to the construction of roads and railways, the Fraser River formed the main travel artery in the Lower Mainland. Thus, the *Fort Langley Journals* present a picture of considerable activity on the river, especially at the time of the annual salmon runs. Numbering in the thousands, people from as far away as Squamish, Nanaimo, Chemainus, Cowichan, Saanich, Sechelt, Songish, Klallam, Skagit, and Nooksack canoed up the Fraser to trade at the fort, and in many cases, to fish for salmon in the Lower Fraser Canyon.

ESTABLISHMENT OF THE FIRST FORT LANGLEY

The central Fraser Valley's river location, its proximity to the sea, its location north of a probable international boundary, and its untapped fur resources eventually drew the Hudson's Bay Company to explore the area. On 24 November 1824, James McMillan and 38 other employees of the Company left Fort George (now in Oregon) in search of a site for a fort in the Lower Fraser Valley. McMillan followed a traditional First Nations route. Upon reaching Boundary Bay, his party journeyed up the Nicomekl River, portaged to the Salmon River, and boated down the Salmon River and into the Fraser. McMillan made contact with a number of Native people, and these encounters were noted in a journal kept by his clerk, John Work. The Natives the party met were described as members of the "Cohoultits" Nation, who at that time were living "in their winter villages in the little rivers." McMillan and his party spent several days exploring the riverfront of the Langley area, then returned to Fort George to make their report.

In 1827, a second party, again under McMillan's leadership (including several men who had accompanied him in 1824), travelled north to establish a post. The party quickly established a fort on the Fraser River near what is now the centre of Derby Reach Regional Park. A cairn just north of Allard Crescent and across the road from the Regional Park's "heritage area" parking lot marks the approximate location of the fort. Unfortunately, wave action and currents along the riverbank appear to have eroded much of the original site. Riverine erosion may also have undermined one of the two or three cemeteries established outside the fort's palisade.

Initially, the fort provided support to the Company's coastal trade and assisted in combating American competition. The fort's later purposes were to supply the Company's interior posts with trade goods, equipment, and locally grown produce or harvested foodstuffs. The post would also receive furs for shipment to the Company's markets overseas. The Company accordingly established a farm on a fertile prairie inland, near the site of modern-day Milner. The farm's produce served the

Company's own needs and accompanied the fort's preserved salmon to Hawaii and other Pacific Rim markets.

By the late 1830s, the Company recognized that the fort was vulnerable to flooding and located too far from its farm on Langley Prairie. The Company determined to relocate the fort farther upstream on a higher piece of land. A new post was thus established at the site of the current reconstructed fort in 1839. The new post burned in 1840 and was immediately rebuilt. At least two cemeteries were established in conjunction with the relocated fort.

Governor Douglas Takes Oath at Fort Langley, 1858

The Company's post at Fort Langley achieved global attention briefly in 1858 when gold was discovered on the bars of the Fraser River. Thousands of eager prospectors streamed into the area in search of the precious metal, and the fur trade post rapidly assumed a role as staging ground and provisioner. A shantytown peopled by Americans, British subjects, Europeans, and Chinese suddenly emerged outside the fort's palisade. Fears that American influence might lead the United States to annex the territory caused James Douglas, the Company's former chief factor and then-governor of Vancouver Island, to assert British claims over the territory, an action later legitimized though an act of the British parliament. British Columbia was subsequently proclaimed a Crown colony in a ceremony in the Big House at Fort Langley on 19 November 1858.

With the creation of the crown colony, a new civil administration was established on the mainland. Intentions were announced to create a capital city at Derby, near the site of the Hudson's Bay Company's first fort. Construction was authorized for a number of public buildings, including a courthouse, a jail, a church and vicarage, and a military barracks. The officer in charge of the Royal Engineers (Col. Richard Clement Moody), however, recognized the deficiencies of the site, and convinced the government to move the capital to New Westminster. The buildings at the Derby townsite were subsequently demolished as settlers mined them for their lumber and as riverboat crews cut them up for firewood. Only the Anglican Church of St. John the Divine survived, being moved to Maple Ridge in 1882. The shantytown along the riverside beneath the fort also disappeared as the miners moved upriver or left the colony to pursue other opportunities.

SETTLEMENT AND DISLOCATION

Farmers and other settlers gradually acquired lots in the Derby townsite through pre-emption, a system through which European settlers could acquire title to crown land by staking and registering a claim and then making "improvements" to the land over the next few years. European settlement also had an impact farther upstream as lands formerly claimed by the Hudson's Bay Company passed into other hands. The decline of the fur trade and competition from newly arrived farmers and merchants led to the sale of the Company's farm by auction, beginning in 1878. A decade later, the Company moved its store from the fort to the emerging village of Fort Langley, not far from the steamboat landing that had long since rendered the fort's fur brigades obsolete.

In addition to marking the start of the Gold Rush, the year 1858 was also significant for the Kwantlen people, for this was when they began to lose much of their traditional territory. While the colony's newly knighted governor, Sir James Douglas, had opened the mainland to settlement by

Kwantlen Village on McMillan Island, c. 1900

Europeans, he had also begun to provide reserves for its indigenous inhabitants. Later administrators were less generous than Douglas (who never completed his allocation of reserves), and the Kwantlen were ultimately awarded five small reserves, the one on McMillan Island being the largest. The Katzie were also awarded five small reserves, including one encompassing the village at the mouth of Yorkson Creek.

The reserve system established first by the colonial government, and continued by the federal and provincial governments, was part of an evolving strategy to assimilate First Nations people into what became a larger population dominated by settlers of European origin. The Kwantlen and Katzie, like other First Nations populations in the province, were encouraged to adopt Christianity, to speak only English, to leave their communal longhouses in favour of single-family dwellings, to abandon hunting and gathering in favour of settled agricultural life and the wage-based economy, and to embrace all other aspects of European life and culture.

The Roman Catholic missionaries and government officials placed in charge of this process appeared to enjoy considerable success in their endeavours. By the late 1890s, Father Eugene Chirouse had built a small but elegant church in the centre of the Kwantlen village on McMillan Island, and the cedar plank longhouses that American artist James Alden had painted in 1858 had been replaced by single-family wood frame houses. At the turn of

the century, many Kwantlen and Katzie were devout Roman Catholics, and the Department of Indian Affairs was able to note that the inhabitants of the Langley and Katzie reserves "follow farming chiefly for a living." A surveyor's map of the Fort Langley area, amended in 1893, shows five fields on McMillan Island, including a potato field. Two of these fields were located just north of the channel separating McMillan and Brae islands.

Some of this apparent change, however, was superficial, and it was certainly short-lived. Most Stó:lō people have long ceased farming, and the churches that once dominated their villages have in many cases been abandoned. Although cattle are still grazed by one family on McMillan Island, the nature of that agricultural activity is essentially non-commercial. In recent years, many aspects of traditional Native culture have reasserted themselves, and senior and local governments now consult with, rather than dictate to, local First Nations.

In the mid-nineteenth century, the Kwantlen and Katzie leadership were well aware of what was happening to their people's culture and became concerned about their loss of lands. In 1864, the chiefs of both the Kwantlen and the Katzie joined other Stó:lō leaders in petitioning Governor Frederick Seymour to ensure that their people would have sufficient land to meet their needs. Similar petitions, some addressing land claims, others speaking to fishing concerns and other issues, were directed to the colonial authorities and to the provincial government that succeeded them in 1866, 1870, 1874, 1875, 1902, 1914, and well into the twentieth century. In the early twenty-first century, however, Stó:lō (including Kwantlen and Katzie) land claims still remained unresolved.

In the 1870s and 1880s, Native people were relegated to the periphery of Fraser Valley society. The agricultural potential of the Lower Fraser Valley began to be better understood. Increasing numbers of settlers arrived from Europe and eastern North America, taking up "unused" land for agricultural purposes or acquiring lots for commercial purposes near the riverboat landing in the evolving village of Fort Langley. Initial settlement tended to be near the river (the area's only transportation route) and on natural prairie lands. Settlers who arrived later often faced the back-breaking task of clearing the forestlands that lay farther inland and on higher and generally less fertile ground. Men such as William Emptage, Kenneth Morrsion, and John McIver were among the earliest settlers in the north Langley area, having elected to remain there upon retiring from their positions with the Hudson's Bay Com-

Monahan Homestead near Murrayville, c. 1890

pany. Families such as the Inneses, the Michauds, the Annands, and the Warks were among the first to take up prairie lands lying farther from the river.

For those who could not acquire naturally cleared land, the task of establishing a foothold

was immense. Massive cedars and firs and thick undergrowth covered much of Langley throughout the 1800s. In the absence of transportation to move timber to markets, the forest cover was generally worthless and was often felled and burned or simply burned where it stood. The stumps that remained were simply ploughed around or removed with stumping powder. Prosperity was often slow to come to farmers on the uplands, and their homes and outbuildings were often small in comparison with those of their more fortunate neighbours on lower-lying properties.

Murrayville, c. 1924-28

DEVELOPMENT OF VILLAGE CENTRES

As settlement moved inland from the river and away from Fort Langley, additional village centres began to emerge. These typically developed at a major crossroads, and ultimately featured a church, a general store, a hotel, a post office, and a blacksmith's shop. Murrays' Corners (later called Murrayville) was the earliest of these new centres, having begun near Paul and Lucy Murray's farm (pre-empted in 1874) where the New Westminster and Yale Wagon Road (later known more simply as the Yale Road or the Old Yale Road) intersected with the trail to Fort Langley. Given its distance from Fort Langley and the availability of land at the time, the village acquired a cemetery of its own in 1891. At its height in the early 1920s, the village featured two churches, a blacksmith and feed shop, a livery stable, two hotels, two general merchants, a toy factory, and a community hall that also served as the seat of local government. (Langley had incorporated in 1873 and had established its first town hall in Fort Langley.)

The development of Murrays' Corners had been made possible by the growth of a road network throughout Langley. Although in many cases little more than trails, these early transportation routes allowed settlers to penetrate the lands south of the river and to establish the farms that became the life-blood of the community's fledgling commercial centres. The advent of the Yale Road led to the development of a hamlet where the road met the trail to the United States. The crossroads, known as Shortreeds' Corners, featured a general store and post office and the township's first customs office (in the picturesque home of settler William Vannetta).

Much of Langley's early development owed its success to poorly paid Asian labour. Many Chinese men had come north from California during the Fraser River and Cariboo gold rushes, while others had come to British Columbia to work on the construction of the Canadian Pacific Railway (CPR). Although many returned to China, others remained, taking up whatever work they could find in an increasingly white and anti-Asian society. Chinese workers were often employed in land clearing and assisted in the construction of much of the Yale Road. Similarly, Chinese, Sikh, and Japanese labourers were a significance component of the labour force in early logging and milling operations throughout the township. While the Chinese and Sikh population tended to be seasonal, dozens of Japanese settled in what they hoped would be permanent homes in Langley's Fern Ridge, Coghlan, and West Langley districts between the two world wars, taking up land disdained by the European population and establishing successful berry farms.

Though the growth of the township's local road network was seen to be important, settlers and speculators longed for the arrival of a railway. The first transcontinental railway, the Canadian Pacific Railway, reached the coast in 1885. With its nearest station in Port Haney, across the river from the

Derby townsite, the CPR had little direct impact on Langley, other than increasing the rate of arrival of settlers from the east. Not until the twentieth century did the Great Northern (1909), British Columbia Electric (1910), and Canadian Northern (1915) railways arrive in the township.

The Great Northern Railway had two stations in the township: one in the emerging village of Aldergrove, the other at Lincoln, near Murrayville. Property owners and businesspeople complained that the line had more interest in serving transcontinental rather than local traffic, though its several branch lines led to the emergence of commercially viable sawmills in the southern half of the township (including the Fern Ridge Sawmill near Campbell Valley and the Fern Ridge Shingle Mill in Aldergrove).

Shortreed General Store, 1890s

The Canadian Northern Railway (later amalgamated into the federally owned Canadian National Railways) had a stop at Glen Valley and a station in Fort Langley, but apparently served local needs little better. It was left to the British Columbia Electric Railway (BCER), with its multiplicity of tiny stations from Vancouver to Chilliwack – including nine in Langley – to ensure the easy movement of passengers and goods. The "Interurban," as the railway's service came to be known, operated until 1950, carrying milk, butter, and other produce from local family farms to markets in the city.

The coming of the BCER led to an increase in both urban and rural growth as land speculators, developers, and intending settlers turned their attention to the township. New Westminster's F. J. Hart acquired extensive land holdings in the easternmost part of Langley, facilitated the growth of the village of Aldergrove (with a hotel, telephone exchange, meat market, general store, blacksmith's shop, churches, and other amenities), and offered small acreages for sale to would-be apple orchardists. Unlike the villages of Fort Langley and Murrayville, Aldergrove never acquired a cemetery of its own. Deceased members of the community were often buried in the Aberdeen Cemetery just east of the township's border in what was then the neighbouring Municipality of Matsqui.

Land companies were also active in other areas of Langley. In 1910, land promoter Charles Edward Hope developed schemes for extensive subdivisions to the south and west of Fort Langley village, a vision not fully realized until the development of Walnut Grove as a major community in the 1980s and 1990s. The village of Milner grew up where the BCER met the Langley Trunk Road (later called Glover Road) and the road to Murrayville (today's 216th Street). With its Methodist church (later United and still later Orthodox), Anglican church (later moved to Otter), blacksmith's shop, general store, post office, and bank, Milner served the many farms that emerged on the fertile lands formerly occupied by the Hudson's Bay Company's farm.

Langley Prairie (today's City of Langley) was the last of the township's historic villages to emerge. Located where the BCER met the Yale and Langley Trunk roads (as well as the road to Cloverdale and Ladner), Langley Prairie developed as a child of the automobile age. Its central location, accessibility by car, and range of amenities (such as banks, medical services, hotels, cafés, agricultural supply shops, and a theatre), ensured its pre-eminence among the township's urban centres.

Langley's growth through the first half of the twentieth century was for the most part slow and steady. Though many ablebodied men failed to return from the Western Front following the 1918 Armistice, the federal government's Soldiers Settlement Board facilitated the efforts of others to take up land and earn their livings on small agricultural holdings. The construction of the first Trans-Canada Highway (now known as the Fraser Highway) through Langley in the early 1930s was followed by the construction of the Patullo Bridge in 1937. Both projects improved travel between Langley and New Westminster and increased the importance of Langley Prairie in the commercial life of the Lower Fraser Valley.

During the Second World War, many Langley men enlisted for service in the Canadian armed forces, and Langley Prairie's Athletic Hall became a training facility for the local militia. After the war ended in 1945, the community experienced modest growth as servicemen and women returned from overseas, married, and began to raise families. More rapid population growth, however, did not occur until the late 1960s and early 1970s, largely spurred by the construction of Highway 1 through Langley in 1964.

The growth then experienced in the Greater Vancouver area led to the establishment of the Agricultural Land Commission in 1972. Much of the agricultural land in Langley was suddenly in the Agricultural Land Reserve, dictating that future growth be directed to land of lesser agricultural significance. The majority of Langley's recent residential growth has therefore occurred in areas such as Brookswood, Aldergrove, the Murrayville uplands, Walnut Grove, and Willoughby. Industrial and commercial development has occurred in West Langley, south of Milner (the Mufford Industrial area), north of Aldergrove (the Gloucester Estates), and, more recently, in Willowbrook. Concern about the community's rate of growth has led to considerable public debate, and caused the Township to undertake a number of initiatives to protect the area's environmentally sensitive areas and heritage resources.

Cemeteries and Society

IT is often said that only two things are inevitable: death and taxes. But while western society seems to talk about taxes freely and without inhibitions, any discussion about death, funerals, and cemeteries often makes people uncomfortable. Given our society's focus on youth, consumerism, and beauty, this should not be surprising. Cemeteries are reminders of our own mortality, and this is something that we are often loath to acknowledge.

Earlier generations knew death as a constant companion. Infant mortality was high, epidemics were frequent, and it was common for even seemingly healthy adults to die prematurely and unexpectedly. People attended funerals frequently, and cemeteries were part of their daily lives. Families purchased plots to accommodate the remains of all their members, ensuring that although individuals might die, the family unit would ultimately be reunited.

Until the early nineteenth century, responsibility for the provision and maintenance of cemeteries in the western world was seen exclusively as a public responsibility. Cemeteries were owned and operated by local councils, churches, and individual families. By the early 1830s, however, entrepreneurs became increasingly aware of the potential profits that cemeteries afforded. The privately owned cemeteries that subsequently emerged were designed to be spacious, sanitary, and picturesque. They solved many of the problems relating to over-crowding and poor sanitation experienced in the previous century; moreover, they appealed to middle-class values, and became highly desirable places of interment.

In the mid-1800s, visits to cemeteries became a common family activity on Sunday afternoons. Regular graveside visits helped the recently bereaved come to terms with their loss. But Victorian cemeteries were designed and operated not just as places to dispose of the dead. They also served as botanical gardens, public open space, and schools of instruction in sculpture, architecture, and public affairs.

Highgate Cemetery, mid-1800s

Mount Auburn Cemetery, mid-1800s

Victorian attitudes toward cemeteries vanished in the early twentieth century. The horrors of the "war to end all wars" pushed aside the old social order and severed the bonds of inhibiting convention. People lived increasingly for the present and tried not to think of death. Inconspicuous "lawn cemeteries" replaced the icon-laden burial grounds of the previous century. Ostentatious funerals and the old, formal code of mourning were cast aside. One no longer visited a cemetery to explore it in depth, but rather to visit and tend the graves of particular individuals and then to leave, sometimes as quickly as possible.

Today, cemeteries are at a crossroads. Regrettably, some of British Columbia's oldest and most significant burial grounds have been cleared of their monuments and turned into passive parks. In others, some of the most impressive Victorian monuments have been removed and laid flat, to cut the costs of maintenance. Municipal cemeteries, traditionally operated as a public service, now find themselves without adequate funds for "perpetual care" and face increasing competition from the private sector.

Seventy-five years after the appearance of the first lawn cemeteries, however, there is strong evidence that society is once again beginning to face the

reality of death. Recent years have seen the development of local hospice societies and formalized grief-counselling services, while the private sector in particular is beginning to offer the types of burial options people demand, rather than those prescribed by long-outdated and highly restrictive municipal bylaws.

Although many people prefer not to give the matter much thought, cemeteries continue to serve valuable social functions. At a purely utilitarian level, they provide a safe, managed place for the disposal of human remains. Further, they provide acres of valuable green space in the urban areas that have now grown up around them. Their lawns and driveways beckon walkers, joggers, and cyclists. Some even provide a refuge to birds and small animals.

Cemeteries also assist in developing a sense of community. Their monuments testify to the evolving values of their community and offer a record of the lives of those who came before. They document the religious beliefs of former generations and testify to the ethnic makeup of the community. Each and every cemetery is as unique as the community that created it.

For those with an interest in history and genealogy, cemeteries provide a valuable database of information. The monuments within them record the names and dates of birth and death of a community's pioneers, chronicle family relationships, document mortality rates, and illustrate changing aesthetic preferences. In the case of some individuals, inscriptions on cemetery markers may be the sole evidence of their fleeting time on earth.

A cemetery's greatest contribution to society probably lies in its role as a place where we come to terms with the reality of death. In the mourning process it is important to have a place to visit those who have passed before us, a place to reflect and even commune. A known gravesite, preferably marked, facilitates our coming to grips with loss and assists us in getting on with the business of living.

Cemetery Design

MOST of Langley's current residents trace their origins to the countries of Western Europe, and it is from there that many of the community's early burial practices originated. In Western Europe, organized cemeteries have long been part of civilized life, considerable effort often having been expended in ushering the dead to their final place of rest, whether in barrows, stone-lined tombs, or simpler earthen burials.

By the latter days of the Roman Empire, the Christian Church often guided burial practices. Royalty, the nobility, and high-ranking clerics were buried in or under their cathedral or parish or abbey church. Elaborate tombs often marked their place of interment. Commoners, who formed the vast majority of the population, were generally buried in unmarked graves in their local parish churchyard, their graves facing east in anticipation of the Second Coming of Christ. The common people not only lacked the means to provide themselves with memorials; according to the beliefs of the time there was no need. Peasants and townspeople knew their station and were content with an anonymous burial. It was enough that their burial places were known to God and by those who survived their passing.

Knowledge of an individual's place of burial might last a generation or two, after which time it was easily forgotten. By then little material evidence remained, vegetation having covered the grave mound that had long since subsided. New burials took place in the churchyard, and if an earlier inhabitant was disturbed, it was a simple matter to inter another corpse above them or to gather the few remaining bones and place them in a common charnel house. Graves were constantly used and reused, the level of the churchyard gradually rising to accommodate a never-ending supply of human compost.

This recycling of burial plots served communities well, as long as population levels and rates of mortality remained relatively constant. But by the mid-eighteenth century, Western Europe, then in the throes of the First Industrial Revolution, began to experience urban population growth of unprecedented proportions. New towns and cities emerged to house industrial workers. Living conditions were often primitive, crowded, and unsanitary. Life expectancies were short, infant and child mortality rates being particularly high, as is evidenced by the following nineteenth-century children's rhyme:

Grandmother, Grandmother,
Tell me the truth.
How many years am I
Going to live?
One, two, three, four …

12

While rural residents living in the English county of Rutland in the mid-1800s might expect to live to thirty-eight, the life expectancy of a Manchester mill worker was just seventeen. In Western Europe's cities, high population levels coupled with high death rates led to an untenable situation. The mediaeval churchyards that had for centuries served local residents became utterly inadequate for the burial needs of the new industrial age.

As new interments were made, recent burials were disturbed prematurely, well before decomposition had reached the stage where it was safe, decent, or agreeable to take the remains to the charnel house. As bodies were buried in increasingly shallow graves, one body stacked upon another, decaying corpses proved an irresistible attraction to wandering dogs. Horrific stories were told of offensive odours, infestations of rats, and even epidemics occurring as a result of the situation.

Reform-minded civic authorities eventually recognized the need to ban burials within highly populated areas and began to look for alternatives. In eighteenth-century Italy and France, men of the Enlightenment recognized the ill effects of urban interment. In England, writers such as J. C. Loudon, a pioneer in cemetery design, advocated the creation of large, landscaped cemeteries outside city limits, a type of burial ground later referred to as the "picturesque rural cemetery."

By 1790, the French National Assembly, then in the hands of the Revolutionaries, passed a statute making it illegal to use the churchyards of Paris for further human burials. Four rural cemeteries were created outside the city limits, including the famous Père Lachaisse, now home to the graves of many distinguished French statesmen, intellectuals, and artists.

By the early nineteenth century, the rural cemetery movement had spread to Britain, where it truly took flower. Large civic or private cemeteries, often on higher ground, threaded with picturesque winding drives and punctuated with romantic group-

Highgate Cemetery Looking Toward St. Paul's, mid-1800s

ings of ornamental trees, arose throughout Britain. Many were segregated on the basis of race, religion, or organizational affiliation. Glasgow soon had its Necropolis, and by 1839 London had its Highgate, Norwood, and Kensal Green cemeteries.

The rural cemetery movement was quick to take hold in North America. Boston outlawed urban interments in 1823 and opened its Mount Auburn Cemetery in 1832. Philadelphia's Laurel Hill followed in three years' time, and New York's Green-Wood Cemetery opened in Brooklyn nine years later. In Canada, two rural cemeteries were developed in Toronto: the Necropolis in 1855, and Mount Pleasant in 1876. Farther west, Victoria's quintessentially romantic Ross Bay Cemetery saw its first burial in 1873.

For those who lived in nineteenth-century cities, cemeteries became far more than simply places to dispose of society's dead. They became places for education, reflection, and recreation. They were often the objects of Sunday afternoon excursions, families leaving the confines of the city to perambulate along their walks, amid their monuments, and under their trees. Published guidebooks assisted them in their walks, documenting the lives and virtues of the principal inhabitants, and identifying the trees – often from around the world – that peppered the landscape. In many cases families even picnicked within their bounds, something that many would find unthinkable today.

Laurel Hill Cemetery, Philadelphia, mid-1800s

Although the rural cemetery movement took hold of urban North America, its influence in the truly rural areas of Canada and the United States was significantly less. There, people continued to bury their dead in cemeteries just outside what were once the town limits, or in churchyards or cemeteries near their local churches. The dead were laid in plots according to a simple grid, with few, if any, intervening walks or plantings. Where they were truly isolated, families sometimes buried their dead in family plots within the confines of their farms.

These were the type of cemeteries that most clearly influenced the design of Langley's two early municipal burial grounds. Such cemeteries were often simple in the extreme. Many were fenced (to prevent wandering livestock from doing indignities to the dead), and most had tended lawns, especially as the nineteenth century advanced. "Improvements," echoing the landscape features of the rural cemetery movement, such as ornamental trees and shrubs, and perhaps a curving drive, were occasionally introduced, but small town cemeteries generally lacked the pretensions of those found in larger population centres.

Advocates of the rural cemetery movement often called for single monuments to commemorate the various members of a family. In a very few instances, a single monument memorialized a num-

ber of families. Tradition, however, called for single stones to mark the graves of single burials, or, at most, those of a husband and wife. Monuments proliferated until, in some eyes at least, the cemeteries serving the cities became congested with a plethora of tombstones, picket fences, iron enclosures, and stone curbing.

THE TREND TO LAWN CEMETERIES

By the mid-nineteenth century, landscape designers were acutely aware of what they saw as a problematic situation. They responded to what they called "clutter" by advocating an alternative form of cemetery design. Variously called the "landscape-lawn," the "garden-park," or the "lawn-park" cemetery, this solution to the problem of cemetery design opened up the landscape. "Lawn-park" cemeteries such as Cincinnati's Spring Grove Cemetery featured a pastoral rather than a picturesque landscape dominated by vast expanses of lawn punctuated by a few stands of trees. In these cemeteries family monuments were encouraged, and individual monuments, curbs, posts, and enclosures were discouraged.

In Langley, no overt movement arose to redesign the Township's cemeteries, but even so, the 1898 Cemetery Bylaw gave the cemetery commissioner (who was no landscape architect) the authority to prohibit the installation "of any fences, railings, monuments, tombstone, tablets, trees, or shrubs which he may deem unsightly or offensive, or which may be injurious to surroundings or adjacent lots, to the paths or walks in the Cemetery."

By the 1920s, many of North America's nineteenth-century cemeteries were becoming full, and some, lacking the revenues that new burials provided, elected to lower their standards of maintenance. As attitudes toward death began to change, many cemeteries ceased to be the object of civic pride. A new concept for cemetery design, the "lawn cemetery," also known as the "memorial park," began to gain popularity.

The lawn cemetery was an American invention and reflected an entirely new way of thinking about death. The Victorians had faced death head-on and were comforted by strong religious beliefs. But after experiencing the horrors of the First World War, western civilization appeared to lose much of its faith in the Creator. Certainly, society became less romantic and far less sentimental. Death became something to be denied, or at least something to be downplayed. The cemeteries of the new age were therefore designed to be less obvious and less filled with emotion. They became examples of efficiency, where the number of burials was to be maximized and maintenance costs were to be minimized.

Proponents of the lawn cemetery contrasted their vision for the cemeteries of the future with those that already existed. On 31 December 1918, the *New Westminster Columbian* reported plans for a new lawn cemetery in Burnaby. Representatives of Ocean View Burial Park – which opened the following year – put forward a vision of "ornamental trees and shrubs, beautiful flower beds, and smooth winding walks and drives, with a total absence of the usual somewhat ostentatious reminders of the harvest gathered by the grim reaper."

Ocean View Burial Park, Burnaby

In keeping with this new philosophy, thousands of lawn cemeteries quickly took form. As their names suggest, such cemeteries were characterized by vast expanses of lawn, unbroken by paths, lofty trees, vertical monuments, or fences. Where trees were planted, they were placed not to obscure the openness of the view. Evergreens, which require less maintenance than deciduous trees, became the favoured form of vegetation. Shrubs such as boxwood, junipers, or cedars were carefully clipped to assume anything but a natural appearance. Monuments were invariably horizontal and rectangular and set flush with the level of the lawn (to facilitate mowing and to eliminate the need to trim around them).

Prior to the advent of the lawn cemetery, it was possible to identify a community's past leaders and people of means simply by looking at the sheer size and opulence of their cemetery monuments. This is no longer the case. The proliferation of lawn cemeteries, with their standardized flush-mounted monuments, has been a great equalizer, requiring people of wealth and stature to be content with markers indistinguishable in size and impact from those of lesser means and lower community profile.

Although the lawn cemetery concept remains at the core of contemporary cemetery design, it has recently undergone some change. Cemetery authorities in British Columbia are increasingly responding to the high incidence of cremation by offering scattering gardens or columbaria to receive cremated remains. The family plot is making a comeback, with private-sector operators allowing brick-walled gardens and vertical monuments in areas once intended solely as lawn cemeteries. Group mausolea are being built, mainly for south European and Chinese consumers. New architectural and landscape solutions – such as high-rise mausolea and columbaria – are also being considered, though none have yet been implemented.

Men and Monuments

JUST as the design of cemeteries began to change with the dawn of the industrial revolution, so did the character of the monuments within them. Writing in the mid-1700s, poet Thomas Gray portrayed a typical English churchyard as a highly romantic haven:

> Beneath those rugged elms, that yew tree's shade,
> Where heaves the turf in many a moldering heap,
> Each in his narrow cell forever laid,
> The rude forefathers of the hamlet sleep.

But even as Gray was writing, many an English churchyard began to be transformed. The Age of Reason placed a new focus on the identity of the individual, while the Industrial Revolution gave rise to a new middle class. The two developments increasingly gave people the motivation and the wealth with which to provide themselves with a stone monument upon their deaths.

The earliest known tombstones, in Britain at least, seem to date from the late 1600s. For the next two hundred years British tombstones generally took the form of a tablet, that is, a vertical stone monument several inches thick and up to four or five feet high, generally with a curving top. Monuments in predominantly Roman Catholic countries, on the other hand, often assumed the form of a cross.

Such monuments were carved from whatever type of stone was in the neighbourhood and generally bore the name and dates of birth and death of the person commemorated. They could also indicate a place of birth and the name of a spouse, and they generally contained a religious or moral text, either to offer comfort to fellow Christians or to comment on the virtues of the deceased.

Langley's earliest "tombstones" were likely made of wood, and some were probably cruciform, marking the graves of the predominantly French-Canadian, Native, Kanaka, and mixed blood servants of the Hudson's Bay Company. For the most part, such markers were not a precursor of the tombstone styles that would eventually proliferate in the township. Instead, it was the British tradition of stone tablets – brought to North America by Puritan, Presbyterian, Anglican, Quaker, and other British settlers – that eventually made its way to the Fraser Valley. Thus, when the Fort Langley Cemetery opened for public use in the early 1880s, the first marker installed was a tablet marking the grave of Scots-born settler Robert Mackie.

Tablet-form monuments proliferated in Langley's cemeteries throughout the 1880s and 1890s, most manufactured by monument makers in New Westminster or Vancouver. Virtually all were carved from marble, which was probably imported from Vermont or Italy. A few bear their makers' signatures, a practice that was common earlier in the century. Some take the form of Gothic arches and boast other Gothic elements, such as quatrefoils or trefoils, in their design. Most contain decorative carved motifs, such as clasped hands, pointing fingers, and doves. A few incorporate elegant floral decoration. Inscriptions are generally incised, with several lettering styles sometimes appearing on a single stone.

Stones dating from the 1880s and 1890s generally reflect the overtly Christian beliefs of those whom they commemorate and of those who oversaw their purchase. These stones recall lines of scripture or recite excerpts from well-known hymns. They offer words of consolation and call upon the reader to have faith in God and in the Resurrection of the dead. Yet while monuments from this period reflect the community's near-universal belief in a Christian God, few take the form of a cross. The Langley of the late nineteenth century was overwhelmingly Protestant, and the Latin crosses so often associated with Christian burial were generally considered a Roman Catholic symbol. The community's few Roman Catholics preferred to be buried among fellow believers in St. Peter's Cemetery in New Westminster, rather than among Protestants whose claim to salvation seemed spurious at best.

Obelisk and Pedestal-style Monuments,
St. Peter's Cemetery, New Westminster

By the early 1900s, the stones erected in Langley's cemeteries assumed a new form and conveyed less information. Made of red, grey, or black granite (probably imported from New Brunswick or Scotland), the stones of the early twentieth century were rendered in a variety of obelisk and pedestal-like forms. They recorded names and dates but often failed to record information of a genealogical or religious nature. These types of monuments were utilised in the province's more urban cemeteries a decade earlier, but appear to have been slower to reach the Fraser Valley.

By the early twentieth century, the technology used to create monuments had also changed. Where an earlier generation of craftsmen had hewn their monuments from a block of rough-cut stone, those who worked in the early 1900s may have bought pre-cut and pre-polished "blanks" into which they sandblasted inscriptions and a few stylized decorations. This was both cheaper and more efficient than the old method of working rough stone entirely by hand. Insofar as these monuments were four-sided and often quite tall, the particulars of several family burials could be accommodated on a single stone marking a large family plot.

In the 1920s, the form and materials of cemetery monuments changed once again. A greater variety of monuments became available, rendering generalizations about their form difficult. Thick, squat, and roughly hewn grey granite tablets (sometimes called "screens" and perhaps drawn from quarries on Texada and Granite islands) were among the most common stones in this period. Like the stones of the early twentieth century, they bear little information: just names and dates, and perhaps a line with a simple epitaph such as "At Rest" or "Gone But Not Forgotten." Unlike earlier monuments, these stones often bore inscriptions in raised lead lettering, rather than carved into the stone itself. Other styles of monuments, including more highly finished, squat granite tablets, were also common in the 1920s.

A decade or so later, American monument makers introduced an array of massive, newly styled monuments to the market: benches, table tombs, porticoes, and human-form sculptures. These proved unpopular in British Columbia, not only because of costs, but also because of the advent of the lawn cemetery.

During the 1930s and 1940s, low-lying concrete ledger stones with low, stamped concrete plaques at their heads became common in both the Fort Langley and Murrayville cemeteries. Many have since been removed, having cracked as the graves beneath them collapsed over time.

By mid-century, Langley's Cemetery Bylaw rendered the highly polished, black granite tablets that emerged in eastern Canada during the 1940s unusable in the township. Instead, the flush-mounted, sandblasted, black and grey granite plaques that first made their appearance in the mid-twentieth century became the most common monuments in Langley's cemeteries. Although municipal regulations also allowed flush-mounted bronze monuments, these were more expensive and, hence less frequently used.

The stone or bronze flush-mounted monuments required by municipal bylaws were initially rather plain, relying largely on stock images and motifs for their decoration. More recently, however, such monuments have become more diverse, despite the limitations placed on them by cemetery regulations. Cemetery monuments now display a greater individuality, with the interests, background, and beliefs of the deceased being reflected in their design. A few older motifs such as lambs (symbolic of youth and purity) and sheaves of wheat (a Slavic symbol representing eternity) have now reappeared.

Other motifs that have recently appeared are less obscure and generally non-religious: a Rolls-Royce emblem, motorcycles, a rifle crossed with a hockey stick, maple leaves (often found on veterans' markers), freight trucks, sports cars, a locomotive, fishing scenes, soccer balls, a grand piano, and even a coiled snake. Whereas religious or sentimental texts were common in the late 1800s, contemporary survivors have inscribed their loved ones' monuments with secular phrases such as "Gone Fishing," "Play on," and "See You in the Movies."

Mortimer's Monumental Works, Victoria, c. 1910-15

With the possible exception of the creators of the ledger stones of the 1930s and 1940s, Langley has never had monument makers of its own (save for the artisans of the Hudson's Bay Company who doubtless produced the long since lost wooden markers in the Derby and Hudson's Bay Company cemeteries). Instead, Langley residents have traditionally turned to artisans and manufacturers in New Westminster, Vancouver, Victoria, and, more recently, Richmond to meet their monument needs.

The oldest known stone monument in Langley marks the Fort Langley grave of Robert Mackie. It is made of sandstone, probably quarried on British Columbia's Haddington Island and likely carved by either Robert Foster or John Mortimer, both of Victoria (the only early British Columbian stone cutters known to have worked in sandstone). Subsequent markers of the 1880s and 1890s are known to have been the work of John Mortimer of Victoria and Alexander Hamilton of New Westminster. Mortimer's signature appears on Alexander Murray's 1884 marble tablet; Hamilton's appears on the Mary Cushan Houston, Richard Henry Holding, James James, William and Isabella Vannetta, and Robert McKee monuments in the Fort Langley Cemetery, and on the Sarah Brousseau monument in the Hudson's Bay Company Cemetery. A number of unsigned monuments in the Fort Langley and Murrayville cemeteries are also probably by Hamilton.

By 1897, Alexander Hamilton had formed B.C. Monumental Works, with premises on Columbia Street in New Westminster. Six years later, Hamilton had several competitors in the younger city of Vancouver: the William Hamilton Manufacturing Co., Samuel McClay, McDonald and Maroney, J. McIntosh and Sons, and perhaps others. By 1911, these firms had been joined by several others, all of Vancouver: Patterson and Chandler, William N. Bertram, Keart and Allen, William N. O'Neil, John B. Newall, and W. C. Thorson. A dozen years later, Hamilton's B.C. Monumental Works had established a branch office in Vancouver and Alex McLennan had opened the Art Monument Company and the Burnaby Monumental Works was in operation on Kingsway. By the mid-1920s, monument making was no longer the exclusive preserve of northern Europeans. In 1926, T. Takahashi was carving monuments for Japanese customers from his works on Vancouver's Powell Street. His business appears to have lasted just three years.

The number of monumental works continued to grow in the 1930s, with John Forster, Joseph Coupland, the Independent Monument Co., Galtano Marchesi, Cecil E. Willey, the Kingsway Monumental Works (run by the Stephanini family), and a few others joining the ranks of firms based in Vancouver. Several of these firms operated from premises on Fraser Street, conveniently located across the road from Vancouver's sprawling Mountain View Cemetery.

By this same time, the New Westminster office of B.C. Monumental Works had closed, but Westminster Monumental Works had opened in its stead. It is impossible to state which of these firms were most

Advertisement for B.C. Monumental Works, c. 1920-30

frequently used by Langley residents (signed monuments having gone out of style), but it seems likely that the Vancouver firms received a greater share of Langley's trade as transportation improvements made the city more easily accessible.

Population growth in the Fraser Valley probably encouraged James Westaway to leave his employ with the Art Monument Company and open his Westaway Monumental Works in New Westminster in 1935. The 1940s saw bronze monuments grow in popularity, facilitated by the opening of Burnaby Bronze Memorials Ltd. during the Second World War. But by 1960, both of New Westminster's monument works had gone out of business, perhaps the victims of an overcrowded area of endeavour.

By 1985, directories listed a number of firms in Surrey as having entered the monument making business. These included the Surrey Monument Company and Melody's Memorial Markers. The Ornamental Bronze Company of Richmond also became a major supplier of bronze memorial plaques.

In the late 1990s, the number of monument makers working in the Lower Mainland had decreased markedly when compared with the number operating mid-century. In the early twenty-first century, the principal suppliers to Langley customers included the Art Monument Co. (a division of the First Memorial Group), W. R. Chandler Memorials Ltd. (established in Vancouver in 1908), Melody's Memorial Markers Ltd., and the Surrey Monument Co. Computerized and other contemporary technologies now permit a range of designs limited only by the imagination of the customer, with portraits of the deceased increasingly being incorporated into monument designs.

Funeral Services

IN Europe and eastern North America prior to the nineteenth century, virtually all responsibility for funeral preparations lay with the family of the deceased. People generally died in the comfort of their own home, amid family and friends, rather than in a hospital. There were no undertakers, so it fell to family members to wash and lay out the body, to procure a coffin, and to convey it to the church for the funeral ceremony. Friends would carry the deceased to the grave. In isolated communities this pattern remained the norm well into the 1800s.

In Britain – the source of many of British Columbia's funerary practices – the professional undertaker did not appear until the 1830s. Often trained as a carpenter or joiner, he assumed many of the functions that had formerly been the responsibility of family members. Bodies were prepared for burial by the undertaker and then coffined, generally in the family home, where

English Rural Funeral, c. 1872

they then lay in state (often not embalmed) for as much as a week prior to the funeral being held. The undertaker subsequently supervised their removal to the church and their eventual interment.

Funerals in the cities of Victorian Britain could be opulent affairs. Burdened by grief, bereaved families were easy prey for rapacious undertakers, who offered services that families did not need and could ill afford. By the mid-1800s, British middle and upper-class funerals became grand theatrical spectacles. Feeling they had to impress the neighbours, families often purchased hardwood coffins with gilt or silver hardware, hired professional mourners, and purchased memorial cards and black kid gloves as mementoes for friends who attended the funeral. Deceased family members were no longer borne away in wagons, but rather in urn-crowned hearses drawn by teams of splendid, ostrich-plumed horses.

In nineteenth-century Britain, however, rural funerals were much less grandiose. While residents of the new cities quickly embraced the services of professional undertakers, people in the countryside often continued much as they had before, with families and communities rather than paid "professionals" seeing to their funeral needs.

In nineteenth-century British Columbia, the pattern was repeated, though urban funerals on the West Coast never attained the same levels of ostentation as they had in Britain. Further, few immigrants appear to have arrived with the express intent of becoming undertakers. Instead, early British Columbian undertakers usually entered their field by chance. Operating at first solely as woodworkers or furniture makers, they were the logical people to turn to at a time of bereavement. In many communities, no one else could readily make a coffin, and the provision of supplementary funeral services became a natural extension of their work.

English Urban Funeral, c. 1914

Residents of the province's larger communities often had access to the services of a professional undertaker by the late nineteenth century. But smaller communities, and rural ones in particular, lacked the population base to support such a specialized service. There the bereaved either had to engage an undertaker from a larger centre or improvise. Langley was no exception. During the reign of the

Hudson's Bay Company, burials were likely taken care of by the Company's skilled woodworkers. With plenty of coopers and carpenters within their ranks, the Company's servants and their families would have been supplied with coffins with ease.

Coulter and Berry's General Store, Murrayville, c. 1901

After the fort closed, local residents and merchants were forced to provide these services themselves. In turn-of-the-century Murrayville, Coulter and Berry's high-wheeled delivery wagon served as the local hearse. The store's male staff prepared coffins as required. Mourning cloth was stocked in the store. It seems likely that the firm's Fort Langley store served a similar function. However, since Fort Langley was more accessible (by paddle-wheeler) to New Westminster, early residents there may occasionally have called upon the services of a professional undertaker. In the Glen Valley district, Mrs. Eliza Cornock served as the local mortician until professional services reached Langley in the mid-1930s.

EARLY FUNERAL SERVICES

Precisely when the township's residents began to rely on the services of funeral directors from New Westminster is uncertain. It is known that when Murrayville resident James Livingstone was buried in 1903, his relatives hired a horse-drawn hearse from Vancouver to convey his remains from

Sharon Presbyterian Church to the cemetery. They no doubt felt that this arrangement would be far more dignified than Coulter and Berry's wagon, but fate determined otherwise. The day of the funeral was rainy, the flimsy hearse got stuck in the mud on the hill, and the undertaker's two delicate little horses were unable to extricate it from the mire. In the end, storeowner J. W. Berry leapt into action. The coffin was unceremoniously transferred from the hearse to the wagon, which then completed the journey to the cemetery. The story was one that Berry loved to tell, and he always concluded by remarking how Livingstone would have viewed the fiasco, "Its too bad Jim was in the coffin. He sure would have enjoyed a mix-up like that."

Municipal records suggest that undertakers' services were being used on a regular basis by 1910, but probably only for the provision of coffins for the indigent. By then, the Fraser River had been bridged and the Old Yale Road from New Westminster had been repeatedly upgraded. Langley Township Council minutes indicate that the Township dealt with New Westminster undertaker William Ellery Fales on a regular basis for the provision of coffins for indigent residents. In 1910, for example, Fales was paid $26.50 for a coffin for the late Mrs. Tyson, and he received similar amounts for coffins for Henry Barclay Josephs in 1912 and for John Draggan in 1913.

In 1912, the Township paid for the funeral of a man identified as S. Guiseppe (probably Guiseppe Matale, a B.C. Electric Railway Company employee) and attempted to recover its costs from the company. After a protracted process, the Township eventually received $2, far less than the $60 that had been spent on Guiseppe's inquest and burial. Interestingly, it does not appear that hearses were being used for such burials, $8.50 having been paid to the Murrayville Livery Company for the services of a wagon in conjunction with the Guiseppe burial.

New Westminster's earliest undertakers were W. E. Fales and David Murchie. Murchie advertised himself as an "undertaker and furniture dealer" and advised that "country orders" would be attended to promptly. In warm weather, this was undoubtedly a good thing. Extremely cold weather could also present challenges. Mary Wark Starr recalled one memorable incident: "I remember overhearing my mother tell a story Dr. Marr had told her of the mother of a patient of his, who repeatedly pled with her dying daughter, 'Do try to hold on, dear. We can't bury you while the ground is frozen and you know you won't keep till spring.' Dr. Marr was horrified!"

Advertisement for D. Murchie, c. 1895

By 1911, W. E. Fales had brought his sons into the business. Shortly afterwards, a third undertaker, Samuel Bowell, opened his parlour in New Westminster. A fourth firm was in business by 1930, operating under the name of the Paterson Funeral Home. Paterson's advertisements proclaimed that the firm employed a "lady assistant" in an effort to calm any uneasiness that people might have felt about the way in which their female loved ones might be handled. Paterson's subsequently (c. 1933) appointed Cecil Brinnen as their Langley representative.

According to the late Bill Poppy, prior to the mid-1930s, families usually assumed direct responsibility for the provision of undertaking services for deceased relatives. If the decision were made not to purchase a coffin, family members or neighbours skilled in carpentry would generally construct one. Alf Trattle, who was born in Fort Langley in 1911, remembered carpenter William Souter as a highly accomplished coffin maker who crafted receptacles for the village's dead well into the twentieth century. With a coffin in hand, it was left to the family to lay out the remains. These would rest in the coffin in the family's parlour until the day of the funeral, when a horse-drawn wagon, such as Coulter and Berry's, would be used to convey the remains from the home to the church and then to the cemetery. By the early 1930s, a locally owned motor vehicle, or possibly even a motorized hearse from New Westminster, might be substituted for the wagon. With only a single, weekly newspaper published at this time, families relied on word of mouth – and later the proverbial party line – to disseminate information about their bereavement and the funeral to follow.

Advertisement for Paterson's, c. 1933

Langley's early Asian minorities had funeral customs of their own and likely undertook many of the arrangements without assistance from their European neighbours. When Tong Fong died in Langley Prairie in 1918, fellow Chinese men probably took charge of his remains, quite possibly conveying them to Vancouver for burial. The Township has no record of the burials of Shizuko Oishi, Masaru Ikegami, or Chiyoko Sugimato, three Japanese children who died in infancy in the community of Coghlan in 1916 and 1917. They too, were likely taken to Vancouver for burial, though unlike Tong, their remains would not have been disinterred after a period of years to be shipped back to Asia to lie beside the bones of their ancestors. Nor does history record what happened to the bodies of two early

Punjabi immigrants – Radu Singh and Teloo Ram Singh – who died in Murrayville in 1915-16. The fate of Nama (or Numo) Ram Singh, who died in Milner in 1932, is better understood. Local fellow Sikhs apparently took charge of the arrangements. Oral histories have recorded how Numo's remains were anointed with butter, spices, and raisins; placed on a funeral pyre; and cremated in his field.

Numo's Sikh funeral apparently created quite a stir, though curiosity and sorrow rather than fear or outrage may have been the emotions prevailing at the event. The cremation may even have given some residents cause to think about how the funeral customs of mainstream society were beginning to change. Cremation was then becoming increasingly common in British Columbia's larger urban centres. Langley was about to get an undertaker of its own, and funeral practices and cemetery design were about to undergo fundamental change.

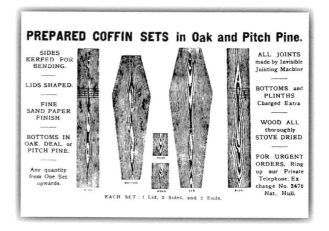

Plans for a Traditional English-style Coffin, early 1900s

LANGLEY'S FIRST FUNERAL HOME

By the early 1930s, Murchie's had left the funeral business in New Westminster, their place being taken by Columbia Funeral Services. Even by this time there were no undertakers operating in Surrey, Langley, or Abbotsford, so the New Westminster firms continued to increase what was initially a meagre hold on the Fraser Valley market. Columbia, however, must have realized there was a growing market to be tapped in the central Fraser Valley, insofar as they opened a branch "funeral home" in Langley Prairie in 1936.

The new funeral home was located in the old O'Neill house, on the site of what is now a series of shops on 204th Street, across the road from Langley City Hall. Funerals arranged by the firm were held either from the funeral parlour or from a church, depending on the wishes of the family. With the opening of the funeral parlour, the older practice of keeping the remains in the family home until the day of the funeral ceased altogether. The advent of the funeral home, like the lawn cemetery, was an import from the south and quite antithetical to the British traditions that had hitherto shaped the province's funerary practices. Further, by the 1920s, American-style caskets were largely replacing the tapered coffins that had previously been the norm in rural British Columbia and which continue to be used for burials in the United Kingdom, even in the early twenty-first century.

The opening of a funeral home in Langley Prairie had other repercussions. Bowell and Son must have taken note of Columbia's move, opening a new home of their own in nearby Cloverdale a few years later. In New Westminster, the Fales family, which had formerly enjoyed a small but continuing trade in Langley, left the funeral business sometime in the late 1930s, leaving the field entirely to their competitors.

Advertisement for Columbia, late 1930s

Columbia's first manager in British Columbia was English-born dairyman turned electrician Arthur Charter. Subsequent managers included W. J. Coles, E. A. Thomson, Bill McMillan, and A. L. Anderson. The firm enjoyed a virtual monopoly in Langley for its first twenty years. Competition finally arrived in 1956 when J. M. Kampf

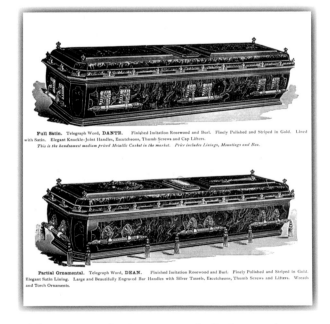

Advertisement for American-style Caskets, early 1900s

opened the Langley Funeral Home, at 202nd Street and the Fraser Highway. Additional competition appeared the same year, when the Memorial Society of British Columbia was established to offer low cost and simplified funerals in the face of alleged price gouging on the part of some of the province's funeral directors. Services offered through the society, whose offices were located in Vancouver, often took the form of memorial services rather than funerals, followed by simple cremations.

In British Columbia, cremation was initially an urban phenomenon, made popular by members of the province's social and economic elite. Poet Pauline Johnson, who died in 1913, was among the first prominent Vancouver residents to choose cremation over in-ground burial. Yet the practice was slow to come to the Fraser Valley, perhaps in part due to the innate conservatism of the population, but also due to the lack of a local crematorium. There were also those who disapproved of the practice on religious grounds, believing that cremation was inconsistent with belief in the bodily resurrection of the dead, a viewpoint still subscribed to by the Roman Catholic Archdiocese of Vancouver. The Anglican Church, on the other hand, has taken a different view, a nineteenth-century bishop of Manchester arguing that it would present little more difficulty "for God to raise up a body at the Resurrection … out of elementary particles which had been liberated by burning, than it would be to raise up a body from dust, and from the elements of bodies which had passed into the structure of worms." By the turn of the millennium, the concerns of social conservatives appeared to have waned, with over 82 percent of dispositions in Langley being conducted through cremation.

The consolidation of funeral services in the Fraser Valley, which began in the 1960s, may have made cremation services more accessible. By 1960, the new Langley Funeral Home operated in affiliation with Henderson's, a regional chain of homes. A. L. Anderson assumed responsibility for Columbia's Langley operations at about the same time. W. D. McMillan was in charge of the Langley Funeral

Home by 1965 and continued in that role when the home began to operate as Henderson's Langley Funeral Home in 1967.

The Old Established Firm

COLUMBIA FUNERAL SERVICE

"THE FINEST FUNERAL CHAPEL IN THE VALLEY"
OUR SERVICE IS COMPLETE
Our services include embalming, hairdressing and complete care, removal from the home or hospital; casket with outside burial case; casket coach, Clergyman's and bearers' car, family car, floral acknowledgement cards; organist, soloist, use of chapel, slumber room, press notices and our personal supervision of all details.

COLUMBIA FUNERAL SERVICE
(J. F. Stephen)
Langley Prairie W.D. "Bill" McMillan, Mgr Phone 205

*Advertisement for Relocated Columbia
Funeral Home, 1950*

Like other funeral homes, Henderson's expanded its range of services in the early 1970s. Under McMillan's management it began to offer "memorial stones and bronze plates," affording its customers the benefits of one-stop shopping. In 1976, Columbia Funeral Services, the old, established firm, closed its Langley operations. Although it continued its business operations in New Westminster, Columbia's closure resulted in Henderson's securing the largest share of the Langley market. Local competition did not reappear until twenty years later. Personal Alternatives Funeral Services and First Memorial Services opened branches in Aldergrove in the late 1990s, serving customers primarily in the eastern part of the township.

In more recent years, other funeral businesses have emerged in nearby municipalities, offering a complete range of bereavement services, including funerals or memorial services, flowers, on-site cremations, bronze and granite monuments, and, where directly operated by a cemetery, burials. Though none of these businesses are located in Langley, many area families are attracted by the comprehensive nature of their services.

In Langley, as elsewhere in the province, the nature of memorialization also changed as the century drew to a close. Traditional funerals, with the deceased in attendance, fell by the wayside, replaced by "simple cremation" and "celebrations of life." Emphasis shifted away from mourning, one Vancouver daily newspaper retitling its obituary page to "Remembering." Memorial services are often casual affairs, the constricting black suits of a former age being replaced by more comfortable wear, and laughter often accompanying tears. Rather than send sympathy cards, friends of bereaved families can now post messages of condolence on funeral home websites. The "visitations" held prior to a funeral, still common in eastern and central Canada, are a rarity in the West, and the "dedication" of monuments is largely confined to people of the Jewish faith. Memorialization also occurs outside cemeteries, as roadside shrines – their increased popularity perhaps inspired by the 1997 palace-gate tributes to Diana, Princess of Wales – appear at the sites of accidents and other tragic deaths.

Floral Tributes for George McDonald, 1927

FRAIL MEMORIALS:
THE CEMETERIES OF LANGLEY

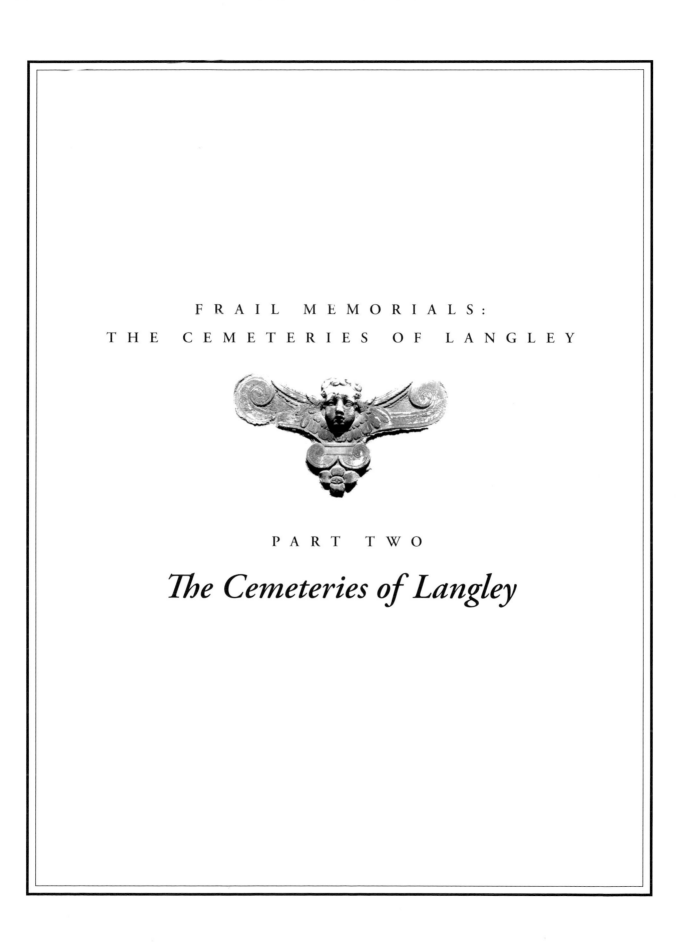

PART TWO

The Cemeteries of Langley

First Nations Burials

LANGLEY was the site of several permanent and seasonal Stó:lō villages. Most of these appear to have been located along the Fraser River or on its several tributaries. Several of these sites were apparently abandoned prior to the establishment of the first Fort Langley in 1827.

Prior to their introduction to Christianity, the Stó:lō generally "buried" their dead above-ground in cedar plank boxes. These were elevated on poles or set in trees. A single box, or grave house, might contain the remains of several family members. These grave houses were located on the outskirts of the village or at locations farther away. When someone died away from the village, efforts were made to return their body home. If this proved impractical, the Stó:lō sometimes resorted to inhumation (underground burial). Inhumation may also have been used at times of massive mortality, such as during the devastating smallpox epidemics of the late eighteenth century.

Responsibility for preparing the dead for burial generally lay with non-family members, under the supervision of a shaman. The body was washed, wrapped in mountain goat wool blankets, then carried to the grave house. Feasting followed, with the food being provided by close friends and relatives. As the blankets in which the deceased were wrapped were subject to decay, they were changed every few years.

Stó:lō Tree Burials, Fraser Valley

Missionaries were quick to discourage the Stó:lō's traditional burial practices. Under their guidance, the Kwantlen established a cemetery in Maple Ridge on the hill just east of what later became the Albion ferry landing, their land on McMillan Island being too low-lying to accommodate a cemetery. Some members of the band, however, such as Chief and Mrs. Alfred Gabriel and their son, Chief Joe Gabriel, are buried in the Fort Langley Cemetery.

The locations of Langley's pre-Christian Stó:lō burial places have largely been forgotten. One such site may have been on what became the Michaud farm, near the Nikomekl River in today's City of Langley. Speaking in the early 1970s, members of the Michaud family recounted how their siblings had found human bones in the area sometime in the 1880s. The children had played with the bones, throwing them into the air and into the river. According to family tradition, their parents attempted to halt the practice by telling the youngsters that the bones would "sing" if they continued to throw them about. Their parents' warning had the opposite effect, the children hurling them all the more vigorously in an attempt to produce the promised sounds. In the end, their father gathered the bones as reverently as he could, interring them in an undisclosed location.

Another known Stó:lō burial site was located in Fort Langley, near where Hudson's Bay Street meets Francis Avenue. Elsie Plaxton Wark grew up in Fort Langley in the 1890s and remembered the burial site well. Her unpublished memoirs note that "there was a bend in the shadowy road to the fort and at the end of this road was an old Indian graveyard. A coffin was seen resting on two strong branches of a big tree. Millie [Elsie's sister] and I always ran as fast as we could past this eerie place on the roadside when it was dark or even getting dark." The cedar box was still in evidence some twenty years later, and young Alf Trattle passed it often on his forays to the area. Whether the remains eventually fell to the ground or were interred elsewhere has not been recorded.

Derby Townsite Cemeteries

THE Derby townsite cemeteries are perhaps the most mysterious of Langley's many burial places. Just who was buried within them and precisely where they were located is unclear. Even the number of cemeteries in the area remains uncertain.

The Derby area's history of settlement is extremely complex, comprising prehistoric First Nations, the Hudson's Bay Company, the aborted capital and townsite, and finally, farming families of European descent. Early white settlers included Alfred Freeman, who sat on Langley Township's first council, and William Hamilton Edge. Alexander Houston, whose father had figured so prominently in the early history of the crown colony, acquired the site of the first Fort Langley in 1912, building a home that survives to the present. The George Brouse and Ralph James Elkins families settled slightly upstream.

Information received from the late Alf Trattle and members of the Houston family points to the possibility of up to three early burial sites on either side of Allard Crescent. All are within a five-minute walk of the cairn installed in 1946 to mark the site of the first Fort Langley and to commemorate the erstwhile community of Derby. Houston family traditions suggest that one of the cemeteries was south of the former palisade in what is now the picnic area in Derby Reach Regional Park's "heritage area."

Alf Trattle, who had a long familiarity with the area (his stepfather was an early settler at Derby), suggested that a cemetery was located near the site of the milk shed that stands in the park's "heritage area" parking lot. Trattle also recalled another cemetery slightly upstream, on what was the Brouse family's homestead in the early 1900s. Both of these latter sites are now covered with blackberries, and at the time of writing, one was in imminent danger of being lost to the waters of the Fraser River.

These cemeteries likely contain the remains of early employees of the Hudson's Bay Company. Members of the families who subsequently settled in the area may be buried here as well. Few written materials document the inhabitants of these cemeteries, though the records of the Hudson's Bay Company offer a couple of clues. Journals kept by the fort's staff from 1828 to 1831 describe how two early employees, John Kennedy and Pierre Therrien, met their untimely deaths. Therrien was killed by a shot fired from the Company's supply vessel, the *Cadboro*. The shot, fired from a cannon, was intended as a ceremonial salute but appears to have been misdirected. A wad of hard rope yarn fired from the cannon hit Therrien with considerable force, resulting in a fatal wound. Kennedy's death was more prosaic, occasioned by a severe cold caught ten weeks before his death, which was perhaps com-

Site of Derby Townsite Cemetery (Brouse Farm)

plicated by tuberculosis or heart disease. Archibald McDonald recorded Kennedy's demise in two journal entries both dated April 1830:

Saturday 17th. About 3 o'clock this afternoon poor Kennedy departed this world, and Certainly Sooner than his Strength & illness indicated – the day being fine he walked the Gallery for the benefit of purer air and then descended to the kitchen, where he Conversed in the usual way with me previous to my going out to the Garden when I had Some work in hand, but was not many minutes there when the Cook ran to me to Say that he was choacking – the only expression he was able to utter after I entered was "Am Done" and was perfectly lifeless in another minute.

Sunday eighteenth. Very fine day – Had the poor deceased decently buried in the afternoon – Afterwards took Inventory of his little effects which were not great, and disposed of them for the benefit of his woman in conformance with his own desire.

Other servants of the Company – as well as their Native wives and mixed blood children – probably also died at the fort prior to its relocation in 1839. In the absence of a monument making industry in those early years, any markers erected were doubtless crafted in the fort from wood and have long since perished in the damp climate of the lower coast. The question remains as to why there would have been up to three cemeteries in the area. Logic suggests that the two sites nearest the cairn – and therefore nearest the original fort – contain the remains of Therrien, Kennedy, and others closely associated with the fort. The cemetery on what became the Brouse property likely dates from after the fur trade and may contain the graves of early agricultural settlers.

Hudson's Bay Company Cemetery – Fort Langley

AFTER those at the Derby townsite, the Hudson's Bay Company Cemetery in Fort Langley is the second oldest known European burial ground surviving in the township. Located on the grounds of St. George's Anglican Church near the corner of Church Street and Mary Avenue, the cemetery served the burial needs of the Company from sometime after 1839 (perhaps as late as 1850) until at least the 1880s. This cemetery, however, was not the only burial ground used by the Company in the area. An earlier cemetery, no longer in existence, was located at the brow of the hill southeast of the present palisade. Three people are known to have been buried there. Two were apparently adults; the other was a child. All three died before 1858, by which date the cemetery had been abandoned.

The cemetery was all but forgotten by the 1920s. In 1929, however, the three graves were unceremoniously rediscovered when a steam shovel owned by the Canadian National Railways uncovered them while extracting gravel from the pit that then lay at the foot of the escarpment east of the fort site. Jason Allard, a pioneer who was born in the fort, and Fraser Valley historian John Gibbard were summoned by the railway. The two men identified one of the skeletons as that of the wife of trader Auguste Willing, who was said to be the daughter

of a Whonnock chief. Her skull had been flattened in her youth by being squeezed between two cradle boards, as was the custom among high-ranking Stó:lō. The second adult skeleton was identified as that of Louis Satakarata Jr., more commonly known as Rabaska. Rabaska's father was three-quarters Iroquois and accompanied James McMillan on his exploratory voyage to the lower Fraser from the Oregon Country in 1824.

Rabaska accompanied his father on McMillan's exploratory voyage. He returned to the lower Fraser with McMillan in 1827 to help establish the fort. Rabaska's father moved to the fort at some later date. Allard placed Rabaska's death around 1848. According to Allard, Rabaska had married an older woman, much against his parents' wishes. The young man left the fort under a cloud, hoping that his father's anger might abate. Upon his return, however, he was soundly beaten. Rabaska fled into the forest, humiliated beyond all endurance. Placing the butt of his rifle on the ground and the muzzle against his chest, Rabaska pulled the trigger with his toe. His friends found his body, wrapped it in a blanket, and buried him in the little cemetery. When his remains were uncovered in 1929, part of the blanket was still intact, perhaps preserved by the lanolin in the wool. The remains of all three people were subsequently reburied in Fort Langley's municipal cemetery, and the location of their former burial place was gradually forgotten.

Just why Rabaska, Mrs. Willing, and an unknown child were buried where they were, rather than in the Company's larger Fort Langley cemetery, has yet to be determined, unless the new cemetery was not yet opened. Nor is it known why the young son of Sapper Thomas Walsh was buried in neither of these cemeteries. According to tradition, Walsh, who was a member of Col. Richard Clement Moody's contingent of Royal Engineers, buried his son in the sloping ground to the north of the fort, sometime around 1859. The lone grave was moved c. 1914-15 to accommodate construction of the Canadian Northern Railway. As the Hudson's Bay Company's cemetery had long since been closed, young Walsh's remains were likely reburied in the municipality's Fort Langley Cemetery.

Research indicates that the Hudson's Bay Company's Fort Langley cemetery harbours the remains of about two dozen people. Jason Allard reported that twenty-three people were buried in the cemetery, while a story in the *Langley Advance* in July 1949 suggested that the number was twenty-four. A survey of the property conducted in April 1999 using ground-penetrating radar identified twenty-four sites where the ground had been disturbed at a depth consistent with a gravesite.

Although the number of burials in the cemetery has now been determined with a fair degree of accuracy, the identities of those who are buried there has only recently begun to be rediscovered. With no written burial register and only a few extant markers, identifying those interred has proved a formidable task. Research conducted by Bob and Sheila Puls, however, indicates that the cemetery is the final resting place of a multiracial and polyglot society that included Britons, French Canadians, Métis, Iroquois, Stó:lō, and Kanakas.

Only four markers remain. Many early burials were doubtless marked with wooden headboards and, in the case of Roman Catholics, with wooden crosses. Of these wooden markers, only one still

exists, memorializing the infant son of Henry and Eliza Peers, who died at the age of three weeks in 1850. Young Peers's modest headboard, the oldest marker to survive from the cemetery, is now preserved inside St. George's Anglican Church. Another memorial, a wrought iron marker in the form of a cross, is now mounted on the church's front gable. The cross commemorates Katrina, the high-ranking Kwantlen wife of Pion Pion (Peoh Peoh), and perhaps Pion Pion himself, a Kanaka employee of the Company. The iron cross is identical to those found in cemeteries established by the Oblates of Mary Immaculate – a Roman Catholic missionary order – throughout the Fraser Valley and likely dates from after 1861, the year in which the Oblates

Restored Headboard of Peers Infant, 1850

founded their mission in the central Fraser Valley (at Mission). It is somewhat ironic that the cross is now located on an Anglican church, the two faiths being bitter enemies in the mid-nineteenth century.

Two other monuments, both of marble, stand within the cemetery itself. One, a tablet surmounted by a Latin cross, marks the grave of Sarah Brousseau, the wife of Hudson's Bay Company employee Basil Brousseau Jr. The other marks the grave of Ovid Allard, the four-year-old son of Jason and Seraphine Allard, who died in 1884. Jason's father, also called Ovid, served the Company in several capacities. He worked at Fort Langley from 1839, built Fort Hope in 1848, and managed Fort Langley from 1864 until 1874. The senior Ovid is also buried in the cemetery, probably near the grave of his grandson Ovid and other members of the Allard family.

Also likely buried in the cemetery were members of several other fur trade era-families, including the Brousseaus, the Cromartys, the Fallardeaus, and the Pepins; and a number of the Company's Kanaka servants. William Henry Newton, clerk in charge of the fort in the early 1860s, is buried here, as is a sapper of the Royal Engineers who died while surveying the border with the United States in the late 1850s. The death and burial of the latter was particularly poignant, as was recollected by the Rev. W. B. Crickmer in 1874:

> As may be imagined, life in the midst of a great forest, in a climate where gales are of continual occurrence, is one long peril to life and limb; every minute the crash is heard, far or near, of some forest monster; often enough close to the huts of the party – sometimes upon them, when asleep at night, or at work in the day. In one gale a poor sapper was crushed to death by the fall of a pine. His dying wish was to receive Christian burial at my hands. His comrades resolved to attempt fulfillment of his sacred wish. Although the measured distance might be only twenty-four miles, yet the carrying a burden through forest was such an undertaking as none would attempt

save from love, duty, or necessity. At last, late one Sunday afternoon, the little party made its appearance, under Lieutenant Darrah, R.E., who, I believe, has since gone to join his comrades in arms. After the service in a small wooden mission chapel which I had erected up there on the sandspit, we went to the little cemetery belonging to the Hudson's Bay Company, and just outside the fort. After the graveside service I delivered an address to the people – storekeepers, Indians, Chinese, gold-miners, Hudson's Bay Company employees, but especially to the soldiers, who evidenced their deep grief in losing a comrade they loved much. They seemed to feel the address; and no marvel, for what comes from the heart finds its way to the heart.

Long after this event, by the time of Ovid Allard's and William Henry Newton's deaths in 1874, the fort had entered a period of decline. The creation of the crown colony had ended the Hudson's Bay Company's trading monopoly as well as its de facto control of the British Columbian mainland. The Company's farm at Langley Prairie ceased to be profitable and was sold at auction. The fort itself was closed in 1886, its store moving to the village centre that was beginning to form at a nearby steamboat landing. Alexander Mavis, a gentleman farmer from the north of England, acquired the Company's Fort Langley properties in the late 1880s, subdividing them a few years later.

An Anglican congregation was organizing at the time, and Mavis, himself a member of the Church of England, willingly sold its members the cemetery site. Just why the congregation chose to purchase a property encumbered by burials remains unclear. There were few Anglicans interred in the site, but romantics in the congregation may have revelled in the acquisition of a ready-made churchyard. The congregation built a church on the unused portion of the site in 1900, dedicating the structure to St. George, the patron saint of England. The construction of a hall in 1947-48 (to the north and east of the church) resulted in at least one unmarked grave being disturbed, the remains uncovered being described at the time as those belonging to "a tall man." Additional remains were uncovered in 1951-53, during construction of a septic field, and were carefully reburied.

In 1954, with the centennial of the creation of the crown colony looming on the horizon and the prospect of reconstructing a portion of the fur trade post becoming a topic of public discussion, interest in the cemetery's history began to increase. In mid-June, members of the congregation gathered in the cemetery with representatives of the provincial government, members of the Fort Langley Restoration Society, and other community members. A plaque had been installed on a large granite boulder, noting the significance of the site and paying particular tribute to Ovid Allard and William Henry Newton.

Speeches were made and the plaque was unveiled, but the highlight of the gathering was the consecration of the cemetery, which, despite a century of burials on the site, had apparently not been done before. Anglican Bishop Godfrey Gower presided,

assisted by Canon A. Fraser and Rev. Tommy Harris, Rector of St. George's. The consecration followed the ancient rituals of the Anglican Church: the bishop led a solemn procession around the cemetery, his clergy and the laity following as the bishop read from the Psalms. The procession then returned to the boulder for the recitation of prayers, an address, a hymn, and ultimately a benediction.

By the mid-1990s, the significance of the site and the fact of its consecration had largely been forgotten. The church required additional space, and after briefly considering building on the cemetery, the congregation elected to review other options. The church was raised and enlarged with a basement underneath, and a new hall was created on the expanded footprint of the old, leaving the cemetery undisturbed. The project, which was completed using a heritage revitalization agreement with the Township, proved highly successful and was recognized by an Award of Honour from the Heritage Society of British Columbia in 2004. Today the cemetery is in use once again, a memorial garden having been established around the cairn for the deposition of cremated remains.

Plaque Unveiling, 1954. L to R: Bishop G. Gower, E. G. Rowbottom, Canon A. Fraser, Rev. T. Harris

SARAH BROUSSEAU
1889

A small marble cross commemorates the late Sarah Brousseau, wife of Hudson's Bay Company dairyman Basil Brousseau Jr. The stone is one of the most intriguing monuments in the township. Sarah was either Kwantlen or Katzie, and early written records give her Native name as Kleka Ke or Kleka Pierre. The inscription on her stone records her date of death as 1889, at the age of 47. This would place her birth date at 1842. Census records, however, list Sarah as still being alive in 1891, aged 43 (born 1848). The stone itself is also interesting insofar as the Brousseau surname is misspelled as "Brewseau."

Carved by New Westminster monument maker Alexander Hamilton, the stone bears the text "The cross is my anchor," a reflection of Sarah's Roman Catholic faith. Sarah may not actually be buried under her headstone, the monuments in the cemetery having been disturbed at the time the church hall was constructed. That she was buried in the Hudson's Bay Company's cemetery seven years after the opening of the municipal graveyard in Fort Langley suggests that she must have wished to join family members already buried in the older cemetery. A rival tradition suggests that she may in fact have been buried at Derby, possibly on what became the Brouse property (Basil Brousseau's executor was George Brouse), and that the stone was brought to Fort Langley to save it from falling into the river.

COMMEMORATIVE CAIRN
Various dates

A bronze plaque, mounted on a granite boulder, commemorates all the Hudson's Bay Company families buried in the cemetery. It singles out two of the cemetery's most prominent residents: Ovid Allard, builder of the second and third Fort Langleys (whose workforce included Basil Brousseau Sr.), and William Henry Newton, who succeeded James Murray Yale as officer in charge of the fort. The boulder was brought to the site from Surrey's Fleetwood district in 1954, at which time the commemorative plaque was installed and the cemetery consecrated.

Fort Langley Cemetery

THE need for a municipal cemetery was first expressed at the Municipal Council meeting of 5 September 1877, when it was moved by Councillor James Houston and seconded by Councillor Campbell "that the Lieutenant Governor be respectfully requested to appoint a Board of Trustees for the purposes of a public cemetery at Langley."

The colonial government had passed "An Ordinance to Make General Regulations for the Establishment and Management of Cemeteries in the Colony of British Columbia" in 1870. The act was amended in 1877 to ensure that any new cemeteries were located away from populated areas. Whether the provincial government or the Township failed to follow through on the council's motion is unclear, but not until the council meeting of 5 February 1881 was substantive action taken to establish a cemetery in Langley. According to the *Mainland*

Dalgleish Family Plot, c. 1894

Guardian, "It was decided to take immediate steps to procure a site for a cemetery, and Councillors Maxwell, Shaw, and Towle were appointed to a committee to ascertain where an eligible site could be obtained, and report progress at next meeting." Council received the committee's report and agreed to purchase two acres for a municipal cemetery from Fort Langley hotelier and landowner John James Taylor.

The site of the new cemetery was located on the west side of the Trunk Road (now Glover Road) near what evolved to become the centre of the village of Fort Langley. Although the community has since grown to surround the burial ground, it met the Province's locational criteria at the time of its purchase, being established in what was then a rural area. In 1881, the village of Fort Langley, then known as "Langley," was little more than a cluster of commercial buildings between Mavis Street and the steamboat landing on Bedford Channel. For several years the only building near the site was St. Andrew's Presbyterian Church (built in 1885 and a United church since 1925), whose presence lent an air of sanctity to the cemetery across the road.

The site was procured in June 1881 and Councillors Shaw, Maxwell, and Towle were appointed to a committee to make the property suitable for burials. A road (St. Andrew's Street) was constructed south of the cemetery the following summer, and an appropriation of $50 was authorized "for the purpose of clearing the cemetery land." The Township's action was timely, for a burial site was required in early December 1882 to accommodate the remains of the late Robert Mackie, father of the Township's first warden (mayor). Robert Mackie was buried in the cemetery's southeast corner. His grandson Jamie joined him in 1885, and his son James, the former warden, in 1903.

The initiation of burials required the Township to take further action to develop and maintain the site. A contract for fencing the graveyard (in the amount of $36.50) was awarded to J. D. McIver in December 1882. In June 1883, according to Council minutes, "tenders were ordered to be called at the next meeting for chopping the graveyard, clearing the portion of the road in front of it, and ploughing and seeding that portion already cleared."

The Township also took steps to develop legislation to govern the "laying out and management of the Graveyard." Langley's first Graveyard Bylaw received its initial reading on 7 July 1883 and a board of trustees consisting of Reeve (Mayor) John Jolly and James Mackie was appointed to oversee its operation during the current year. Just how the board of trustees envisioned laying out the new cemetery remains unknown, no plans having survived to tell us. It seems highly likely that both Jolly and Mackie were familiar with the principles of nineteenth-century cemetery design, but the layout of the Fort Langley Cemetery owes more to the traditional churchyards of rural Britain and the roadside graveyards of southern Ontario than

it does to the grand, romantic cemeteries that had for half a century proliferated in England, Scotland, and eastern North America. The cemetery lacks the picturesque drives and ornamental plantings found in the Glasgow Necropolis, in London's Highgate Cemetery, or even in Victoria's Ross Bay Cemetery. Instead, the Fort Langley Cemetery was laid out with a single semicircular drive (to enable funeral processions to enter and leave the cemetery without having to turn around), a few straight paths, and a minimum of ornamental plantings. The graves in the cemetery were ultimately laid out in a simple grid of plots with intervening pathways.

By 1888, a cemetery commissioner (caretaker) had been appointed. The identity of the first commissioner is uncertain, though he may have been James Mackie. What is known is that council instructed him in March 1891 "to furnish the Council with a statement of accounts in connection with the graveyard." D. Symington was appointed "Graveyard Commissioner and Caretaker of the Town Hall" in February 1892. (Fort Langley was then the seat of municipal government for Langley Township, and the Town Hall was located on the site of the current community hall.)

Symington was soon instructed to "lay out $10" to plough and level additional land within the cemetery boundaries. He continued in his position until January 1894, when George Rawlison replaced him. James Morton Drummond, who had served as clerk in charge of the Hudson's Bay Company's Fort Langley operations from 1887 to 1892, succeeded Rawlison in 1895. Drummond took his work seriously. In February 1895 he wrote to council to express his concerns about stray livestock wandering through the graves. (A municipal bylaw permitted cattle to run at large from 1 April to 31 October.) Graves lacking fenced enclosures were particularly vulnerable to strolling cattle. Drummond immediately received authorization to draw up specifications for a new fence and to have the work undertaken. Mr. A. Mowat was awarded a contract in the amount of $35 to build the fence.

General View of Fort Langley Cemetery

Early cemetery commissioners were paid an annual salary of just $10. Their responsibilities included digging and closing graves, maintaining the cemetery lawn and plantings, and maintaining the Town Hall. Insofar as lots in the cemetery sold for $6 each in the 1890s, the cemetery generally paid its own way.

Mr. W. Blizard was appointed to the position of cemetery commissioner in April 1896 and was soon instructed by the clerk to ensure that all plots in the graveyard were paid for in advance and that all payments in arrears were collected in a timely fashion. Early cemetery commissioners apparently kept haphazard records, for at a council meeting in July 1896 "the Clerk was instructed to ask Mr. Drummond for a statement of his collections as graveyard commissioner."

Fort Langley blacksmith William John McIntosh was appointed as the Township's new cemetery commissioner in January 1897. McIntosh and the new council apparently recognized that the burial ground's problems were more extensive than had been originally thought. It was soon decided that a survey of the cemetery was required to ensure that fences, and indeed, graves, were located in the proper places. Council was particularly concerned by correspondence from a neighbouring property owner, Charles Edward Hope, himself a surveyor, complaining that the cemetery's fence encroached on his land and advising that the late settler Samuel Titmus had been buried not in the cemetery, but on land belonging to Hope. Council responded by moving both the fence and the grave, and advised Hope of their actions.

COUNCIL TAKES CHARGE

By 1898, Langley's council were truly taking their responsibilities regarding the cemetery seriously. A new cemetery bylaw was adopted in March 1898 and A. H. P. Matthew was appointed cemetery commissioner and hall caretaker, with an annual salary equal to $15 plus 50 percent of hall rental proceeds. In an effort to regularize the cemetery's records, an expenditure of $7 was authorized to procure a supply of 300 cemetery plot receipts. The new bylaw confirmed the cemetery's boundaries, required council to appoint a cemetery commissioner each year (with a salary not to exceed $20), set the cost of plots at $6 each, set aside land "for the burying of strangers and indigent paupers," and established regulations regarding the erection of fences and monuments and the planting of trees by plot owners.

With a new bylaw and cemetery commissioner in place, one of council's next acts was to request that W. J. McIntosh provide a report on which lots he had sold. Council also approved funding for a boat for the cemetery commissioner, presumably to enable him to reach homesteads along the Fraser River and possibly to reach businesses (including undertakers) in New Westminster.

In 1899, council noted a discrepancy between the number of plots sold and the receipts on hand.

Langley pioneers had apparently agreed to buy plots, had buried their dead within them, but had neglected to pay the commissioner for the lots. That same year council established a policy not to allow burials in the "previous portion" of the cemetery, but rather to clear and fence the "outside portion." This led to early gravesites being concentrated on the Glover Road frontage of the cemetery, with later graves located farther west.

By early 1899 it was noted that "brushing" (clearing) was required in the graveyard. Basil Brousseau Jr. (a former Hudson's Bay Company dairyman and one of the earliest settlers in Langley's Willoughby district) was contracted to complete the work for a fee of $147. Shortly afterward, the Township received a garnishee summons from notary Walter Wilkie with respect to any funds they owed Brousseau. The unfortunate Brousseau received just $54.06 from the Township, his creditors receiving the balance.

Council's negative experience with the Titmus burial and the lack of a comprehensive survey resulted in a decision to engage Ernest Albert Cleveland of Vancouver "to survey and lay out the cemetery." The completion of the survey enabled the cemetery commissioner to place iron pipe in the cemetery to mark its coordinates, replacing the inaccurate wooden stakes that had hitherto been used. Shortly afterward, the Township offered Thomas Mufford the sum of $3 compensation for his claim of damages (after a Mufford family grave had been dug in the wrong place). Mufford initially refused the money but ultimately took the payment offered.

Commissioner Matthew does not seem to have been reprimanded but found himself in trouble again when council received a letter from Mrs. E. Maxwell regarding "the state of the cemetery." The Township responded by reviewing Matthew's books and accepted his resignation shortly afterward. J. T. Bramwell succeeded him as cemetery commissioner. Bramwell also appeared to experience difficulties in carrying out his responsibilities. In May 1904, it was recorded in council's minutes, "Council instructed the cemetery commissioner to request Jos. Morrison to remove headstone from Jno. Maxwell's lot, and also to proceed with the collection of accounts due on lots."

TWENTIETH-CENTURY DEVELOPMENTS

In August 1904 the Township's responsibilities regarding cemetery administration became more complex. The Cloverdale Odd Fellows Lodge determined to sell their cemetery at Murrayville to the Township and the offer was accepted. Bramwell resigned his position as cemetery commissioner shortly thereafter and James Allen was appointed in his stead. A second commissioner was appointed to administer the cemetery at Murrayville. The newly acquired cemetery became known as the "Langley Prairie Cemetery" and later as the "Murrayville Cemetery." The older burial ground continued to be called the "Langley Cemetery" well into the twentieth century.

Edward Henry Stanley Smith, an individual sometimes described as an English remittance man, succeeded Allen in his role of Langley cemetery commissioner in 1910. Percy Primrose, Langley's earliest professional photographer, followed him in 1913, and Francis Edgar Fairbourne succeeded Primrose the following year. Council continued to supervise the cemetery commissioners for a number

Fort Langley Cenotaph

of years, despite the existence of two senior staff positions (municipal clerk and engineer) that might have taken on the role. Nonetheless, as the twentieth century progressed, Langley's cemeteries began to be operated in an increasingly professional way, and bylaws were passed that significantly affected the form that the two cemeteries take today.

A veterans' section was established in the Fort Langley Cemetery shortly after the end of the First World War. This section accommodates the remains of Langley residents who served in the Allied forces during the First and Second World Wars as well as the remains of other former members of the Canadian armed forces. The veterans' section is located west of the stone cenotaph (constructed in the form of a Celtic cross) that names the servicemen from Langley who died and were buried overseas during the First and Second World Wars. A stroll through the graves reveals that many young men died in the years immediately following the First World War, succumbing to their wounds not on the battlefields of France and Flanders, but in the arms of their loved ones at home or in hospital among strangers. The cenotaph itself is identical to the cenotaph in the Murrayville Cemetery. Both were funded by public subscription, with returned soldiers Archie Payne and Dr. B. B. Marr leading the campaign. The two monuments were unveiled in April 1921 by young relatives of Langley men who had perished during the war. Langley's tribute to the young men who had died in the "war to end all wars" did not end there. In December 1921, council renamed many of the township's roads in memory of individual soldiers. Memorial maple trees were planted at major intersections, each dedicated to the memory of an individual soldier and each marked by a tall wooden cross. In the early twenty-first century, only four of these trees remained, including three in Fort Langley and one in Milner. The wooden crosses that formerly identified them have long since disappeared. Instead, inscribed bronze plaques now stand beside the trees, identifying each of the soldiers commemorated.

During the 1920s, revisions to the Cemetery By-law reflected the changing tastes of the new century and new attitudes toward death. As newer sections of the cemetery were developed, they became less inviting, and in some ways, less interesting than their nineteenth-century predecessors. By the 1930s, west coast cemeteries were increasingly being redesigned to appear less "cluttered" and more homogeneous. The lawn cemetery movement then in vogue called for a simplification of the landscape and downplayed the monument – the visible reminder of death. The new approach seems to have been widely embraced by British Columbian municipalities. In keeping with a new emphasis on efficiency, Langley's council developed new regulations to establish standards for monuments. Curbs and fences were prohibited, and the only markers allowed were granite or bronze tablets whose top surfaces were laid flush with the ground, to facilitate mowing. In enacting such regulations, the Township was not only responding to a desire to decrease its maintenance costs, but was also echoing the new approach to cemetery design that was sweeping the continent.

As a result of this change in taste, the section of the cemetery near Glover Road – where the oldest burials lie – has a Victorian and Edwardian feel, while the sections to the west reflect the modernizing tendencies of the lawn cemetery movement. The spaces in between are a zone of transition, with a proliferation of flush monuments punctuated here and there by a few more assertive vertical monuments.

The movement toward cremation as a popular alternative to interment has also made its mark in the cemetery. (In 2005, cremations accounted for 71 percent of dispositions in British Columbia.) Pathways that once divided the older part of the cemetery into sections have now been filled in and given over to the burial of cremated remains. Township regulations now permit cremains to share the plot of a previously interred relative, and this has greatly assisted in increasing the capacity of the cemetery.

ROBERT MACKIE
1882

Seventy-five-year old Robert Mackie was the first to be buried in what was initially called the Langley Cemetery (Fort Langley being known as "Langley" prior to the development of Langley Prairie in the early 1900s). Robert was the father of the Township's first warden (mayor) and probably came to Langley with his son James Mackie in the early 1870s. Otway Wilkie, who had recently come to Fort Langley from Ireland, is said to have dug the grave.

Robert Mackie's tombstone is one of the few sandstone markers erected on the mainland. It was probably carved in Victoria. Even in 1882 it was somewhat old-fashioned, looking more mid than late Victorian. The stone's design is laden with symbolism. Much of its inscription is placed on a raised heraldic shield, a design feature intended to create a sense of antiquity. Gathered drapery, representative of mourning, flanks the stone, while a classical pediment defines its summit. As was common in the mid to late nineteenth century, several styles of lettering are used in the inscription.

JOHN and CATHERINE McLEOD
1883 & 1916

This fine marble monument marks the burial place of John and Catherine McLeod, who settled in Langley in 1880. Their farm is now the site of McLeod Athletic Park and Langley Secondary School, at 56th Avenue and 216th Street. John McLeod was a native of Nova Scotia but had spent much of his adult life in Nevada. He died of pneumonia shortly after settling in Langley after falling into the Salmon River while hauling lumber from West's Mill (east of Fort Langley) to build a house. His was the second burial in the cemetery.

John's stone formerly stood upright and was, as its inscription notes, erected by his wife Catherine. Catherine left a space on the lower portion of the stone for her particulars, which were added after her death some thirty-three years later. This stone is notable for the quality of its carving, which can be seen in the bouquet of flowers at its base as well as in the lengthy inscription. The stone is almost identical to Alexander Murray's 1884 monument in the Murrayville Cemetery.

JULIA ROBERTSON
1884

Julia (Sannich) Robertson was the Cowichan wife of Samuel Robertson, a former employee of the Hudson's Bay Company and one of the first men to pre-empt land on the Maple Ridge side of the Fraser River. Prior to moving to Maple Ridge, Robertson operated the "What Cheer House," a saloon at the Derby townsite, and the British Columbia Saloon Company, just west of the Hudson's Bay Company's post in Fort Langley. Maple Ridge had an emerging cemetery of its own by the time of Julia's death, but it was located on private property, and not properly drained. These two factors may have contributed to the Robertson family's decision to have her buried in Fort Langley instead of Maple Ridge.

Julia's monument is among the finest in the cemetery and is very well preserved, being sheltered by a tall coniferous tree. The stone, in the form of a Gothic tablet, is decorated with a trefoil at the top, enclosing a carving of a hand reaching down to lift a bunch of flowers. The hand is that of God, while the flowers symbolize the soul of the deceased being carried up to Heaven.

NARCISSE FALLARDEAU
1888

A marble monument marks the grave of one of Langley's true pioneers, a man who had worked under Chief Factor James Murray Yale in building the second Fort Langley in 1839. His marriage to Tlhepartenate, also known as Helen or Ellen, a Kwantlen woman, resulted in eight offspring. In 1879, after leaving the Hudson's Bay Company's employ, Fallardeau acquired a parcel of prime agricultural land east of West's Creek fronting on the Fraser River. He died just nine years later, at the age of 79.

Fallardeau was born in Quebec and it appears that his survivors were unable to communicate the correct spelling of his name to the individual who carved his monument. (Fallardeau himself appears to have been illiterate.) The stone reads "Narcis Fallerdan." Fallardeau's stone is typical of what one might have found in Quebec at the time. As a Roman Catholic, it was important for his grave to be marked by a cross, rather than by a tablet, a style of monument favoured by Protestants.

MARY CUSHAN HOUSTON
1889

A marble tablet marks the grave of Mary Cushan Houston, spouse of former gold miner James Houston. Mary was a Cowichan woman from Nanaimo who had once been the wife of Chief Casimere of the Kwantlen band. She and her sister were Protestants, an unusual situation in the Fraser Valley, having been converted to Christianity by the famous Methodist missionary Thomas Crosby. James and Mary operated a farm in Fort Langley just east of the Salmon River. The couple had a son, Alexander, who farmed in what is now Derby Reach Regional Park, where his house still stands, opposite the cairn marking the site of the first Fort Langley.

Mary's stone bears a simple inscription without a religious or sentimental text, simply noting her name, age, and date of death. Like the Emptage monument, the stone features the clasped hands motif. A signature in the lower right-hand corner reveals its creator as New Westminster monument maker Alexander Hamilton.

RICHARD HENRY HOLDING
1889

Richard Henry Holding and his wife Isabella were natives of Blackpool, in the English county of Lancashire. The couple settled in Langley in 1874 after a thirteen-year sojourn in Australia. Holding found work as a schoolteacher, and although born and raised in an urban environment, he took up two quarter sections of farmland south of Fort Langley. One of these was just west of where Glover Road met the Telegraph Trail; the other is now the site of the Belmont Golf Course. Holding was 59 at the time of his death.

Holding's monument is a tall, austere marble tablet. Its inscription includes a text from the first book of Timothy. Like several other monuments in the cemetery, the tablet was signed by its maker, Alexander Hamilton of New Westminster.

MAGGIE JULIA ROBERTSON
1891

This low marble tablet commemorates the three-year-old daughter of James and Christina Robertson. James was the second son of Samuel and Julia Robertson. He married Christina Margaret Yates in Hope in 1866. Their daughter Maggie was the first of the couple's four children and the only one to die in childhood.

Maggie's stone is noticeably smaller than others installed in the cemetery at about the same time. This is because it marks the grave of a child, and children's markers were usually smaller than those used on adult graves. The stone is decorated with a carving of a dove with a rosebud in its beak. The dove symbolizes the Holy Spirit; the rosebud, young life. Like other monuments of the early 1890s, the stone bears a brief semi-religious text, proclaiming that young Maggie Robertson has "gone to be an angel."

LOUISA EMPTAGE
1891

Louisa Emptage was the wife of William Henry Emptage, a gardener with the Hudson's Bay Company. After leaving the Company's service, Emptage took up land at what is today the site of the 232nd Street interchange on Highway 1. Louisa was the daughter of a high-ranking Musqueam Native, and had been converted to Roman Catholicism by an Oblate priest who gave her her Christian name.

Louisa's marble tablet is embellished with the clasped hands motif, which symbolized two individuals saying farewell. A careful examination of the carving reveals that one hand is male, while the other is female, suggestive of a husband and wife. The stone bears a lengthy text describing one of Louisa's virtues:

> Her voice was ever soft, gentle
> and low.
> Praising what is best makes
> The remembrance dear.

GEORGE STANLEY BROWN
1894

During the nineteenth and early twentieth centuries, infant and child mortality rates were much higher than they are now. Older cemeteries therefore contain a disproportionate number of burials of the young. These are not always marked, the deceased perhaps not having made a sufficiently strong impact on the lives of their survivors to warrant the expense.

George Stanley Brown was the son of Fort Langley hotel owner Peter Brown. Georgie, as he was known to the family, drowned in May 1894 at the tender age of fifteen months, after falling from the hotel's veranda into the swollen waters of the Fraser River, which was then in flood.

Georgie's stone is particularly interesting, taking the form of a low marble tablet surmounted by a resting lamb, symbolic of young life and innocence as well representative of Christ as the "Lamb of God." The stone is small as the deceased was small. Monuments such as this were probably available from suppliers in the cities but were also sold through mail-order houses such as Eaton's and Sears Roebuck. Sears Roebuck advertised an almost identical monument in its 1906 catalogue for $10.45, a price that included an individualized inscription.

JAMES JAMES
1894

James James was one of Langley's earliest settlers. James was a professional miner from the English county of Cornwall; he had managed mines in Colombia and Australia before mining in California. He moved to Langley in 1869 and took up land on the west side of the Salmon River between what are now 88th and 96th Avenues. His son-in-law and business partner was John Jolly, who later became Langley's sixth reeve. James was seventy-nine years old when he died, a remarkable age at the time.

James's well-preserved stone is an elegant marble tablet, Gothic in form, with a pointed finger motif (representing the hand of God pointing heavenward), set in a Gothic trefoil supported by oak leaves. A series of wild roses runs along the edge of the stone. James's monument bears a lengthy sentimental inscription:

> Dear father thou hast from us flown
> To the regions far above
> We to thee erect this stone
> Consecrated by our love

GEORGE and CHRISTINA CARTER
1895 & 1934

The monument marking the grave of George and Christina Carter is the only true obelisk in the cemetery. Obelisks have a long history; they were favoured by the ancient Egyptian pharaohs to commemorate their accomplishments and to honour their gods. During the nineteenth century, Egyptian motifs found their way into cemeteries throughout the western world. This is not surprising, given the ancient Egyptians' seeming preoccupation with death. The main gate at Boston's Mount Auburn Cemetery and the entrance to the Lebanon Circle in London's Highgate Cemetery were both marked by Egyptian pylons and obelisks. Smaller obelisks had marked family plots in the great urban cemeteries of the mid-1800s, and they remained popular into the early 1900s, a few of them finding their way into small-town cemeteries.

The Carters were well-known Fort Langley residents. George Carter purchased property on 88th Avenue just west of the Salmon River in 1883. The bridge that connected his property with Fort Langley village was for many years known simply as "Carter's bridge."

TOWLE FAMILY PLOT
1896, 1909, 1923, 1937, & 1954

This impressive monument marks the graves of pioneers Wilson and Eliza Towle, their son Stanley and his wife Agnes, and other family members, including Wilson and Eliza's grandson, Adam ("Addie") S. Towle, co-founder of Langley Freight Lines. Wilson and Eliza Towle arrived in Langley in 1871 and built their Commercial Hotel near the end of Glover Road, directly opposite John James Taylor's Fort Langley Hotel. After her husband's death, Eliza started construction of a rooming house near what is now Trinity Western University, but she died before it was completed.

The Towle family monument is four-sided and ideal for marking a number of graves within a single-family plot. The stone was likely erected shortly after Eliza's death in 1909, being rendered in a style favoured during the early twentieth century. Formed from red granite, probably from New Brunswick, the monument takes the form of a tall pedestal surmounted by an urn, a symbol of mourning since classical times.

WARK FAMILY PLOT
1898

The Wark family plot contains the graves of several members of one of Langley's earliest European families. Three other members of the Wark family are buried outside the enclosure: former reeve Robert J. Wark, his brother Samuel, and Samuel's wife, Elsie (Plaxton) Wark. Members of the family buried inside the enclosure include the family's patriarch, Alexander, his first wife, Isabella, their son William, and their son Robert's first two children, Robert and Edith, both of whom died in infancy. Losing two infant grandchildren was tragic enough, but William's death was even more devastating. According to family tradition, William left the family farm in 1898 to work on a fishing boat. On his first night out he slipped on the deck, fell into the river, and was drowned.

The plot is remarkable insofar as it is defined by a wrought iron enclosure with fleur-de-lis decorations. The enclosure, dated 1898, was probably crafted by Alexander Wark, who had learned the blacksmith's trade in Ireland. The modest iron fence has stood for over a century, the handiwork of a father grieving for his lost son and looking toward a day of reunion. Neither William's nor any of the other graves within the plot are marked. Although there is no direct evidence, it seems likely that other family plots in the cemetery were once defined by picket fence enclosures, as was common elsewhere in the province in the late nineteenth century.

SUSANAH YEOMANS
1898

Susanah Yeomans, the wife of West Langley pioneer Charles Yeomans, was buried in the family plot in the Fort Langley Cemetery in 1898. Charles Yeomans and his brother John had both taken up land on 208th Street north of 96th Avenue, just north of what was later to become the community of Walnut Grove, about 1887. Members of the family still lived in the area in the early twenty-first century.

Susanah's monument is the only one of its type in Langley. It is made of cast metal coated with zinc (to retard oxidation). Similar monuments are common in other British Columbian communities, such as Victoria, and were probably produced by the White Bronze Company of St. Thomas, Ontario. The inscription on the marker simply records Susanah's name, dates, and relationship to Charles. Because of its zinc coating, the monument remains in remarkably good condition as it enters its second century.

KENNETH and LUCY (ALLARD) MORRISON
1900 & 1924

Born on the Isle of Lewis in the Outer Hebrides in 1831, Kenneth Morrison arrived in Fort Langley after having travelled overland from Fort Carlton, Saskatchewan, in 1853. The journey was a difficult one, by snowshoe and canoe, and by the time Morrison and fellow Company employee, John McIver, reached the West Coast, they were dressed in rags. Less than enamoured with the Hudson's Bay Company, they deserted their posts, only to be captured by chief trader James Murray Yale. The pair had little choice but to remain in Fort Langley, where they were put to work making barrels under the direction of cooper James Cromarty. Morrison subsequently married Lucy Allard, daughter of Ovid Allard, and appears to have been the first European to pre-empt land on the south bank of the Fraser River.

Kenneth and Lucy's monument is a grey granite pedestal surmounted by a pyramid with semicircular gables. Like many other monuments of its time, the marker rises in three stages, a design feature symbolic of the Trinity.

WEST FAMILY PLOT
1900, 1902, & 1912

The family of Henry West share the distinction of having the largest and most impressive monument in the cemetery. German-born Henry West was one of Langley's earliest industrialists. He arrived in the township in the early 1870s and established a steam-powered sawmill east of Fort Langley, where the creek that bears his name meets the Fraser River. The mill was a success and West used the profits to establish a saloon that he later sold to John James Taylor. The mill was also the site of a short-lived boat building enterprise. West married Louisa Fallardeau, fourth daughter of Narcisse Fallardeau, whose grave is adjacent to the Wests. The couple had eleven children.

The West family monument reflects the family's success in their several endeavours. Crafted from white marble, the memorial echoes the form of an eclectic shrine. The monument rises in stages, culminating in a Gothic canopy supported by four Romanesque columns. The canopy offers shelter to a classical urn, a symbol of mourning. The marker was somewhat old-fashioned when installed; a similar monument was erected in Victoria more than ten years earlier.

JAMES HOUSTON
1902

Few of the hundreds of people buried in the Fort Langley Cemetery lived a life as full or as colourful as that of James Houston. Houston was born in Dunfermline, Scotland, in 1823. He came to North America while still a youth, allegedly in the company of a school chum, Andrew Carnegie. Accounts of his life include references to being shipwrecked, being taken prisoner by Maori warriors, being rescued after having swum to a passing ship, dodging South American revolutionaries and South Seas pirates, being attacked and wounded by Native Indians in the Pende Oreille River valley, and finally, being overtaken and robbed by Okanagan Natives while on his journey north. Other accounts credit Houston with being the first European to trade with the Native population for gold, news of which eventually reached San Francisco, resulting in the Fraser River gold rush of 1858. Houston subsequently made his way to the Fraser Valley, where he took up farming near Fort Langley, remaining on his property until his death in 1902.

James Houston's monument is a grey granite pedestal, similar in design to the Morrison monument. Where the base of the Morrison monument features the family name in large incised letters, the inscription on the Houston monument is raised.

JAMES, JAMIE, and ANNIE MACKIE
1903, 1885, & 1917

James Mackie was a prominent early resident of Fort Langley and one of the signatories to the 1872 petition to the Province to create the Township of Langley. Mackie's pleas, and those of the other twenty-nine settlers who signed the petition, resulted in the Province passing its Municipality Act that same year. Municipal governments were established in both Langley and Chilliwack just twelve months later. Mackie, a native of Banffshire in Scotland, was elected to the post of warden in June 1873 and re-elected in 1874 and 1875. When he died in January 1903 Langley's council suspended its meeting on the day of his funeral so that members could attend.

James's stone marks the grave of his young mixed blood son Jamie as well as his own. Erected just twenty-two years after Robert's, their stone is significantly different. Made from the highly polished grey granite that was then becoming popular, James and Jamie Mackie's marker is a much simpler version of Robert's. It is also a tablet, but it lacks the symbolic ornamentation of the earlier stone. Instead, the marker bears only an inscription, noting the dates of death and ages of those that it commemorates. James's widow, Annie, who was burned to death in her bed in 1917, is buried nearby in an unmarked grave.

WILKIE FAMILY PLOT
Various dates

Henry Wilkie, his wife Alice, and three of their thirteen children – all then adults – emigrated from Dublin to British Columbia in 1887. Wilkie had served as Assistant Registrar General for Ireland, a position largely responsible for the maintenance of records relating to births, marriages, and deaths in that country. The family settled in Fort Langley soon after their arrival on the Pacific coast. Several of Henry and Alice's sons secured prominent positions in the Fraser Valley.

Otway Wilkie, one of the couple's sons, was the first of the family to come to British Columbia and had advised his parents of the opportunities that awaited them on the West Coast. Once in British Columbia, Otway worked as a surveyor, then joined the Provincial Police. He also had a long-time interest in the military and served in the Canadian contingent in the South African War, as well as in the Canadian Expeditionary Force during the years 1915-18. His brother Octavius also became a surveyor, assisted by another brother, Walter, who initially worked as a storekeeper. Henry and Alice's daughter, Janet, who had remained in Ireland at the time of her parents' departure, journeyed to Fort Langley in 1890, eventually marrying William (Billy) Morrison, son of a former Hudson's Bay Company cooper.

The Wilkie family plot is defined by four yew trees imported from England. Yews are found in most English churchyards, a carry-over from pre-Christian times, when yew trees were planted at sacred pagan sites. The yew tree's evergreen leaves symbolize immortality. The monuments that mark the graves within the plot are simple black stone plaques.

MAVIS FAMILY PLOT
1893, 1905, & 1926

A large marker commemorates several members of the Mavis family: Alexander Mavis, a former gold miner who had purchased and subdivided part of the Hudson's Bay Company's property in Fort Langley, his son James, Alexander's wife Mary, and Mary's mother, Sarah Nicholson. Mary died tragically in 1905 after being attacked by her husband, who was then suffering from advanced dementia. Alexander himself died three months later at the provincial home for the mentally ill, in New Westminster.

The Mavis family's impressive stone is one of the cemetery's earliest twentieth century monuments, and represents a clear departure from the tablets that had previously marked the sites of earlier burials. Like other monuments erected at the time, the stone is made of polished red granite (probably from Scotland or New Brunswick), sits on a raised granite base, and takes the form of a modified obelisk or pedestal. The stone was probably sent to a monument maker in New Westminster or Vancouver in virtually finished form. All that the monument maker had to do was add the particulars of the deceased and a few bits of ornamentation. The stone is embellished with a sandblasted ivy motif (symbolic of immortality) and a Masonic symbol (suggesting that Alexander Mavis was a Freemason).

JOHN and ELIZABETH MAXWELL
1915 & 1906

John Maxwell was a prominent early settler of Langley. He was one of the signatories of the 1872 petition for incorporation and served three terms as reeve. Maxwell was born in Ireland in 1838 and immigrated to Canada with his parents at the age of 10. Elizabeth, his wife, was born in the Gatineau area of Quebec in 1852. John met her in Wakefield, Ontario, and convinced her to marry him and move to British Columbia. John and Elizabeth, and her mother and brother, eventually acquired sizeable properties immediately to the south and east of Fort Langley. Elizabeth was the first to die, in 1906 at the age of 54. John followed in 1915 at the age of 79.

The Maxwells' stone is a modified obelisk, worked from polished black granite and set on a stepped base. Its top is defined by four Gothic crockets and may have once been surmounted by a cross. As was the custom in the early 1900s, supplementary text is kept to a minimum, reading simply "At Rest."

ALLARD FAMILY PLOT
Various dates

This large plot was likely purchased by Jason Allard on behalf of his family in the early 1890s. Allard, who earned his living variously as a surveyor, interpreter, and farmer, was born within the palisade at Fort Langley in 1848. He married Seraphine Joseph, a Native woman from Port Townsend, in 1879. The couple had thirteen children, five of whom (Matilda, Helena, Francis, Ambrose, and a still-born child) died young. Seraphine died in 1915, aged 52. Jason outlived her by sixteen years and at the time of his death in 1931 was widely acknowledged as an authority on the history of early Fort Langley. Jason's father, Ovid Allard (1817-74), builder of the second Fort Langley (1839), is also commemorated on the stone, though buried in the Hudson's Bay Company Cemetery a few blocks away. Jason's mother, Justine, who died in 1907, is buried in Jason's plot rather than with her husband, the Hudson's Bay Company's cemetery having fallen into disuse by the time of her passing.

The Allard family monument is a marble pedestal, now coloured a graceful blue-white. Vandals have long since removed the cross that once surmounted it, a symbol of the family's Roman Catholic faith.

TAYLOR FAMILY PLOT
Various dates

John James Taylor was one of the signatories to the 1872 petition to the Province requesting the establishment of municipal government in Langley. Taylor had come to Langley from the Orkney Islands in 1858 and initially found employment with the Hudson's Bay Company as a blacksmith and barrel maker. Upon leaving the Company's service, he acquired extensive property in Fort Langley west of what was then known as the Trunk Road, renamed Glover Road in 1920. Taylor subsequently opened the Fort Langley Hotel and a blacksmith shop. He sold the site of the cemetery to the Township in 1881. Taylor's first wife, Catherine Fallardeau, died in 1874 and is remembered on the family's tombstone, though she was likely buried in the Hudson's Bay Company's cemetery in Fort Langley, the municipal cemetery not opening until a decade later. Taylor's second wife, Barbara Jamieson, who died in 1909, is buried beside him. Other members of the family are also buried in the plot. These include Taylor's grandson, John James Clifford Taylor, who enlisted in the Canadian Expeditionary Force in 1916 at the age of 16, only to be expelled for being underage.

The Taylors' monument is a massive grey granite block set on a heavy stone base, dominating the family plot. The marker bears a thistle motif in raised relief, a symbol of Taylor's Scottish origins. Acanthus leaves, representing peace, support its four corners.

RICHARD and ISABELLA (GUEST) HOLDING
1889 & 1914

Richard Holding is one of the few people in the cemetery who had two monuments erected in their memory. The first must have been installed at his head shortly after his death. The second commemorates both Richard and his wife; it was probably erected after her death in 1914.

The two stones are side by side and a comparison of the two indicates how tastes had changed in the twenty-five years that separate them. The first monument is a traditional tablet; the monument erected after Isabella's death is clearly one of the twentieth century, in the form of a modified obelisk. It is unusual for a marker of this period to contain a lengthy Biblical text, but the Holdings' survivors provided one for both Isabella and Richard.

WILLIAM and MARY (ABERCROMBIE) LAWRENCE
1935 & 1917

Irish-born William Lawrence was one of the earliest settlers on what had formerly been the Hudson's Bay Company Farm on Langley Prairie. William was born in County Langford and had served as a policeman in the Royal Ulster Constabulary prior to immigrating to British Columbia in 1883. He married Port Moody resident Mary Abercrombie, also a native of Ireland, in 1894. The couple had four children: sons William, Glover, and Robert, and a daughter, Margaret, who married Charlie Logan, a member of a farming family with extensive property in what later became the City of Langley. Glover served in the Canadian Engineers during the First World War. William was a remarkable contributor to the life of the community, serving eleven years on Township council and a further fourteen years on the local school board. Langley's schools were closed on the day of his funeral, which featured six honorary pallbearers as well as six active pallbearers.

The Lawrence family plot is marked by a large black stone "screen," surmounted by a cylinder, which, like a circle, symbolizes eternity. The monument dates from a time when the lawn-park cemetery movement – which favoured single large stones to mark the graves of several family members – was in its prime.

BENJAMIN BUTLER and ISABEL DREW (McINTOSH) MARR
1939 & 1936

Langley's much-loved Dr. Benjamin Butler Marr, the community's first and for many years only physician, died in 1939 at the age of 57. His wife predeceased him, dying in 1936 at the comparatively young age of 40. Dr. Marr set up his practice in a home in Fort Langley in 1910. It was there that he met and married Isabel McIntosh, daughter of Fort Langley blacksmith and policeman William John McIntosh. Dr. Marr's practice initially encompassed the entire township, a district of some 120 square miles, with many of his patients served by house calls.

Like hundreds of other men in the community, Marr enlisted in the Canadian Expeditionary Force during the First World War, serving in the Canadian Army Medical Corps. He resumed his practice after the war, ultimately relocating twice, at first near the Five Corners in Murrayville, and later in a large house on the hillside just west of what would later become the site of Langley Memorial Hospital. Both Marr and his wife were extensively involved in a number of community organizations. In reporting his passing, the *Langley Advance* remembered Dr. Marr as "a rare personality [who] carried a smile and a pleasantness for everyone that revealed friendship unexcelled." Isabel Marr was equally revered. Her funeral was described as "one of the largest ever held in the Fraser Valley," the *Langley Advance* reporting no less than 154 floral tributes.

The Marrs' monument belies their importance in the community, being a plain black plaque, mounted flush with the level of the lawn. Though bearing no epitaph, the stone incorporates the scribe and square of the Masonic Lodge and the star of its companion organization, the Order of the Eastern Star.

JAMES CROMARTY
1936

Fort Langley resident James Cromarty was born in the Hudson's Bay Company's post in 1853. His father was William Cromarty, chief cooper of the fort from 1830. James Cromarty was evidently one of the strongest men in Langley. When he died in 1936 at the age of 83, the *Langley Advance* noted: "In his younger days, James Cromarty was known for his remarkable strength. He is credited with having lifted 1300 pounds in a weight lifting contest. On another occasion he walked in from a steamer in Fort Langley with thirteen sacks of flour, each weighing 49 pounds."

A squat grey granite tablet, decorated with stylized flowers marks James Cromarty's grave. Its simple line of text reads "Rest in Peace."

GEORGE C. CARTER JR.
1940

A thick, Gothic-style grey granite tablet marks the grave of George and Christina Carter's son George, who died in 1940 at the age of 56. In reporting the details of Carter's funeral, the *Langley Advance* noted the impressive size of the congregation and that "the fragrance of many floral offerings was especially noticeable."

The stone is an unusually late example of its type, for flush-mounted monuments were more the norm by mid-century. The monument features a cross and ivy motif and includes the text: "Safe in the arms of Jesus."

CHARLES EDWARD and LILY (MAVIS) HOPE
1949 & 1957

Charles Edward Hope was a major figure in Langley during the first half of the twentieth century. His obituary, published in the *Langley Advance* in May 1949, attested to his multi-faceted endeavours, lauding him as a "pioneer, farmer, town planner, financier, architect, engineer, and civic personality." Hope was a Yorkshireman who left his native Bradford for Vancouver in 1888. Initially working as an architect and land surveyor, Hope soon realized that land and resource development might prove more lucrative possibilities. In 1892, he married Lily Mavis, daughter of Fort Langley farmer and landowner Alexander Mavis, thus beginning a connection with Fort Langley that was to last the rest of his life.

Although he had significant business interests elsewhere in the province, Hope built a substantial home, Illahie, in Fort Langley. From there he managed his many business ventures as well as his Deep Creek Farm in West Langley. Hope was a Conservative in politics and held a number of local elected positions. Like many of his contemporaries, he was also a racist, serving as secretary of the White Canada Association and publishing a number of anti-Oriental articles in *Maclean's* magazine. Hope and his wife were strong supporters of St. George's Anglican Church. When Lily Hope died in 1957, she was eulogized as one who "was renowned as a benefactor of nearly every community project."

The Hopes' monument is a black stone plaque that is significantly larger than similar stones in the cemetery. Apart from the couple's names and dates, the marker bears the inscription, "At Rest" and the symbols of the Masonic Lodge and the Order of the Eastern Star.

CAROL LYNN WHITCOMB
1946

The smallest monument in any Langley cemetery marks the grave of Carol Lynn Whitcomb, who died on 4 March 1946, aged just five weeks. Carol Lynn was the daughter of Melvin and Helen Whitcomb, residents of Langley's Armstrong Hill district. Her short life was troubled with ill health. Born with clubfeet, she ultimately died of thymic hyperplasia, a disorder of the thymus gland, which was compounded by a lung haemorrhage.

Carol Lynn Whitcomb's monument is of engraved aluminium and measures just two inches by four inches. It may have been intended as a temporary marker.

ALEXANDER HOUSTON
1950

Alexander Houston was the son of pioneer James Houston and Mary Cushan. When he died in 1950 at the age of 82, he was described by the *Langley Advance* as "one of the most colourful and respected native sons of Fort Langley." What the *Advance* failed to mention was that, as a young man, Alexander's respectability had temporarily been called into question. What was later described as flimsy and circumstantial evidence had convicted him of his grandmother's murder, a conviction that was subsequently overturned. Upon his release from prison, Alexander's reputation was largely restored. He became a well-liked individual and took an interest in the community, particularly in its history. He donated land for a cairn on the site of the original fort and Derby townsite and was a charter member of the Fort Langley post of the Native Sons of British Columbia. During his time with the Native Sons, the organization took an active interest in the preservation of the third Fort Langley and in the 1930s established the township's first museum in the fort's sole surviving building.

A concrete ledger marks Houston's grave. His name and dates are recorded on a concrete plaque. A grey granite pillar stands nearby. It marks the grave of Houston's one-year-old son, also called Alexander, who died in 1917. According to young Alexander's death certificate, his funeral arrangements were attended to by "friends" rather than a professional undertaker, a practice not uncommon at the time.

JOSEPH MORRISON
1963

Joseph ("Joe") Morrison was one of Langley's favourite sons. At the time of his death at the age of 102, he was one of the oldest people in the province. Joe's father Kenneth had worked for the Hudson's Bay Company in the mid-nineteenth century and had the distinction of being the first pre-emptor on the south side of the Fraser River. Joe Morrison was born within the fort's palisade in 1861. During his youth he worked on the Canadian Pacific Railway and as a logger on the lower coast, felling trees in the 1880s in what was later to become the City of Vancouver. In subsequent years he moved to a house just east of Fort Langley, never marrying. The *Langley Advance* later described him as "a man who scorned the company of women all his life." Ironically, a woman is buried next to him.

A simple bronze plaque without any decoration and bearing the phrase "Fort Langley always his home" marks Morrison's grave.

VETERANS' SECTION
1924

In Victorian times it was common for specific sections of a cemetery to be set aside for the use of individual religious or fraternal groups. The cemetery in Nelson, B.C., for example, contains separate areas for the burial of Anglicans, Roman Catholics, Foresters, Odd Fellows, and Masons. In Victoria, Ross Bay Cemetery was similarly divided. After the First World War it became common to designate a section in a cemetery for the burial of veterans. In later years, some cemeteries also allowed the burial of spouses in the same plot as the deceased veteran.

A veterans' section was established in the Fort Langley Cemetery sometime before 1924, when Archie McLachlan died and was the first to be buried there. Fort Langley's Dr. Benjamin Butler Marr was largely responsible for the creation of the veterans' section, having helped to establish a branch of the Royal Canadian Legion in Langley c. 1923. Dr. Marr also led the campaign to fund the cenotaph in Fort Langley and personally created a precinct around it defined by rhododendrons and cedars. A field gun and two machine guns once stood in front of the cenotaph. Today, only the cenotaph, a single rhododendron, and the cedars remain. A visit to this area of the cemetery is particularly poignant, insofar as many of its earliest occupants survived the war, only to die a few years later of their wounds, still in their twenties or thirties. A veterans' section was also created in the Murrayville Cemetery. Identical granite cenotaphs in the form of Celtic crosses dominate both veterans' sections.

ALEXANDER ALLARD
1924

Alexander Allard was one four sons of Jason Allard who enlisted in the Canadian Expeditionary Force during the First World War. Alexander and his brothers were raised on their father's farm, which is now part of the Fort Langley Golf Course. Three saw action on the Western Front. William survived the war and lived until the age of 73. The middle brother, Eugene, was killed at Ypres in 1917. Alexander survived the war, but his health was destroyed in a gas attack. He died in a Kamloops hospital in 1924. Ovid George, the second oldest, did not reach England until shortly before the Armistice and returned to Canada uninjured.

Alexander's monument is similar to those provided to deceased servicemen overseas by the Imperial War Graves Commission (now called the Commonwealth War Graves Commission), being a short granite tablet with a maple leaf carved over the text and a cross below.

JOHN ANDREW BODALY
1929

A grey granite stone marks the grave of John Andrew Bodaly, a Glen Valley farmer. Andrew Bodaly enlisted in the 230th Battalion of the Canadian Expeditionary Force (a forestry battalion) during the First World War. He returned to Langley, where he was murdered in 1929. According to reports in the *British Columbian*, Bodaly and a neighbour, long-time adversaries, had had an altercation at a Canadian National Railways milk stand near his farm. A knife appeared, and Bodaly suffered a grievous wound. Despite being attended by Fort Langley's Dr. B. B. Marr, Bodaly died on the train on his way to hospital. Bodaly's neighbour was arrested by Langley's chief constable, Robert Macklin, and subsequently charged with murder. Over three hundred people attended Bodaly's funeral a few days later.

Bodaly's stone is one of two types of vertical markers found on veterans' graves in the Fort Langley cemetery, taking the form of what appears to be a scroll. Its text is set within a shield and notes his name, age, and date of death as well as his army unit and serial number.

WILLIAM HARVEY BROWN
1937

Generally remembered as "Billy Brown," William Harvey Brown was a well-known Fort Langley character. Brown was born in Parham, Ontario, in 1875 and married Annie Elizabeth Medd in Fort Langley in 1902. He is remembered as one of the foremost carpenters in the district, who built many early barns, houses, and commercial buildings. Brown also operated the Commercial Hotel for a while, after he moved it from its site on the Canadian Northern Railway right-of-way with the assistance of a group of local men, each of whom had apparently been promised a case of whiskey if they could complete the task by the following morning. Like many Fort Langley men, Brown served overseas during the First World War. In 1937, while serving as cemetery commissioner, Brown is said to have dug a grave for a veteran whose relatives subsequently decided to bury him elsewhere. Shortly afterward, Brown himself became ill. A few days later he was buried in the grave he had dug for another.

Like others in the veterans' section of the cemetery, Brown's monument is styled on the tablets designed by the Imperial War Graves Commission after the First World War. In Europe, most such monuments were carved from Portland stone, while in Canada, grey granite appears to have been the material of choice.

WILLIAM ALLARD
1962

A plaque in the cemetery's veterans' section marks the grave of one of Langley's most distinguished soldiers. William ("Billy") Allard was born in 1889, the son of Jason Allard and the grandson of Ovid Allard. Billy's early working life was spent on the paddlewheelers of the Yukon Territory. When war broke out in 1914, he and several dozen other Fort Langley men enlisted in the Canadian Expeditionary Force. Billy saw action in three of the war's most fearful battles: Vimy Ridge, the Somme, and Passchendaele. His courage in the face of fire earned him the Military Medal, which was apparently presented to him by the king at Buckingham Palace. Two of Billy's brothers were not so lucky. Eugene was killed in action at Passchendaele; Alexander was gassed and died six years after the war ended.

Billy's flush-mounted, grey granite stone is typical of veterans' markers of the 1960s and lies near that of his brother Alexander. Their brother Eugene has no known grave and is memorialized on the Menin Gate at Ypres.

Walworth Cemetery

SOUTH Langley's Walworth Cemetery marks the site of one of Langley's lesser-known tragedies. Located on a bluff on the north side of 16th Avenue east of 200th Street, the cemetery contains seven or eight graves. All the burials in the cemetery apparently relate to the pioneering Walworth family.

Prior to 1894, Langley Township was a municipality measuring 10 miles wide by about 10 miles long. Its southern boundary was 2 ½ miles north of the American boundary. It was into the unorganized territory north of the border that a widow, Mrs. Jane Walworth, and her extended family ventured in the 1880s. Mrs. Walworth and her sons Albert, Charles, Jason, James, and Tom each took up adjoining quarter sections. Her daughter, Charlotte, and Charlotte's husband, Jason Samuel Lewis, pre-empted a quarter section to the north of Albert Walworth's property. Another daughter and her husband, a Mr. Van Luvan, took up land nearby in Surrey. Although others also settled nearby, people referred to the area as the "Walworth Settlement."

In September 1888, a smallpox epidemic reached the settlement. Three family members – James Walworth, Mrs. Van Luvan, and Mrs. Jason Walworth – died of the disease and were buried by the family near Jason Walworth's house. Because quarantine had been imposed on the settlement, it was impractical to bury the dead anywhere else. Tradition states that wishing to rid themselves of the disease, the survivors burned their clothes, then walked to a neighbour's homestead for a disinfecting bath and the basics of a new wardrobe. A rival tradition goes a step further, claiming that Jason Walworth's house was also burned, though this is unlikely, as a relative maintained that Jane Walworth continued to live in the house until her death some years later.

Other burials followed: Albert Walworth in 1896, Jane Walworth some time later, and Mr. and Mrs. Lewis in the 1920s. An unidentified infant may also be buried in one of the adult graves. None of the graves were ever marked, unless with wooden tablets or crosses, which have long since disappeared. Some of the graves, however, were enclosed with picket fences, and daffodils were blooming on the spot until the early 1950s. People forgot about the Walworth Cemetery until that time, when plans were initiated to upgrade 16th Avenue. Research undertaken by Alexander Pepin and D. W. (Bill) Poppy resulted in the Township rerouting the road around the graves, the location of which was reconfirmed by the Township using probes in June 1979.

Murrayville Cemetery

LOCATED west of 216th Street on the Murrayville hill, the Murrayville Cemetery is the second oldest of Langley's three municipal cemeteries. The cemetery enjoys an excellent view of the Golden Ears and a number of other mountains north of the Fraser River. The Independent Order of Odd Fellows (Cloverdale Lodge No. 15) established the cemetery in August 1891. The lodge acquired the property (3.2 acres) as a donation from William (Billy) Murray, son of Murrayville pioneers Paul and Lucy Murray, and operated it as a cemetery for the next thirteen years.

Like the Fort Langley Cemetery, the Murrayville Cemetery is simple in design. It is L shaped, the older sections being those to the north, bisected by a driveway lined with mature deciduous trees. The graves in the older section are laid out in a grid pattern, with no ornamental plantings or intervening pathways, the latter having long since been filled in by the Township. The Murrayville Cemetery thus resembles the roadside cemeteries of southern Ontario or the Maritimes rather than the imposing urban cemeteries of the nineteenth century.

The Odd Fellows developed a set of *Rules and Regulations* to govern the cemetery's operation shortly after it opened. The cemetery was to be known as the "Odd Fellows Cemetery." Although it was owned by the Odd Fellows Lodge, burial in the cemetery was open to all. The installation of fences, pickets, posts, and rails was prohibited without the express permission of the cemetery's trustees. Small shrubs and flowers could be planted, but the installation of trees was forbidden. A register was to be kept, itemizing the names, date of death, nationality, and religious affiliation of all those interred in the cemetery. Rates were more competitive compared to those in effect at the Fort Langley Cemetery. During the 1890s, a family plot measuring 17 feet by 9 feet could be had for just $6, the cost of a single plot at the Fort Langley Cemetery.

The Odd Fellows Cemetery sat unused for well over a year. The first person to be buried was John Jackson, a native of Greenock, Ontario, who was killed by a falling tree at the end of 1892. Curiously, the oldest tombstone in the cemetery predates the first burial. The marker in question memorializes Billy Murray's brother, Alexander, who drowned in the Fraser River in January 1884, trying in vain to save a friend. Alexander, known to the family as "Sandy," was originally buried at Fort Langley, but his family had his body exhumed and moved closer to them after the Odd Fellows Cemetery opened.

The Odd Fellows Lodge operated the cemetery until mid-1904, when they wrote to Langley Township Council, offering to sell the property to the Township. Council accepted the offer and

Rules and Regulations

— OF THE —

ODD FELLOWS' CEMETERY,

Murray's Corner, Langley, B. C.

1st.   That this Cemetery shall be called the Odd Fellows' Cemetery.

2nd.   That the Trustees of CLOVERDALE LODGE, No. 15, I.O.O.F., for the time being shall and are hereby constituted the Trustees of the said Cemetery during the time of holding such office, and in the event of such Lodge being closed, then by three Scarlet Members who shall be appointed by the Grand Lodge of British Columbia.

3rd.   That said Cemetery shall never be governed or controlled by any but members of the Independent Order of Odd Fellows.

4th.   That the purchaser of a lot will be entitled to the same rights and privileges in the said Cemetery as any Odd Fellow, save and except the Trustees as aforesaid, notwithstanding that the said Cemetery is an Odd Fellows Burial Ground.

5th.   That the Trustees reserve the right to prepare the grave under their instruction.

6th.   Graves not to be disturbed or bodies removed without the permission of the Trustees or by order of the Court.

7th.   No fences, pickets, posts or rails can be placed in any portion of said Cemetery without the express permission of Trustees, all plans to be submitted to them for approval.

8th.   Small shrubs and flowers may be planted in lots, but no trees will be allowed. The Trustees reserve the right over all lots to plant any such ornamental trees, shrubs, or bushes, as they may think fit, and to remove all shrubs, fence, or posts as they may deem unsuited to the Cemetery, or which have been neglected by the owners of such lots or portions of lots.

9th.   That every purchaser of a lot shall be duly furnished with a proper deed or title to the same, annexed to which the foregoing rules shall be printed and signed by three Trustees.

10th.   That there shall be a Register kept by said Trustees, or under their immediate instructions, in which shall be recorded the names of all original holders of lots or portions of lots, and the names of all deceased persons interred in said Cemetery, with the date and cause of death, nationality and religious denomination, and the said Register shall be produced for inspection on payment of a fee of twenty-five cents.

Odd Fellows Cemetery Leaflet, 1890s

Reeve John McDonald and Clerk J. W. Berry were "appointed to complete the deal." The price eventually agreed upon was $200 and the transfer of funds was completed in October. Interestingly, the sale was contrary to the provisions of the Odd Fellows' own *Rules and Regulations* which ensured purchasers of plots that the cemetery would "never be governed or controlled by any but members of the Independent Order of Odd Fellows."

The property was renamed the "Langley Prairie Cemetery" and a bylaw to govern its operation received first reading in November 1904. Councillors Deans and Crozier examined the cemetery and recommended that the area previously surveyed and then in use be cleared of stumps, logs, brush, and other debris. The new council approved an expenditure of $59.50 to undertake the work.

J. W. Berry was appointed Langley Prairie cemetery commissioner pro tem and directed "to call in all outstanding deeds and papers in connection with the cemetery in order to get the matter in order owing to the fact that all papers in connection therewith were destroyed in the Cloverdale fire." (The Odd Fellows Lodge in Cloverdale burned in 1904.) Berry remained in the post of cemetery commissioner until 1910, when William Ramage succeeded him. Robert Monahan assumed the commissioner's duties in 1913.

Like their counterparts in Fort Langley, Langley Prairie cemetery commissioners were responsible for maintaining the cemetery, selling plots, and maintaining the cemetery records. Once the Township took over, lots at the two cemeteries were priced the same. Plots at Murrayville initially sold relatively slowly: four were sold at Murrayville in 1909, compared to eleven in Fort Langley.

Murrayville's early cemetery commissioners seem to have encountered fewer problems than their counterparts in Fort Langley. Efforts were made to ensure that records were kept from the outset, and unlike Fort Langley, there is no evidence of fences or burials being located incorrectly. Berry's principal problem probably occurred in 1907 when a locust tree planted by Nels Nelson was judged to have "become a nuisance."

In due course, the Langley Prairie Cemetery began to be known as the "Murrayville Cemetery." Generally, those who were buried there had been residents of the Murrayville and south Langley areas. The cemetery also served many late residents of Surrey, given its initial ownership by the Cloverdale Odd Fellows. Residents of the northern half of Langley continued to be served by the Fort Langley Cemetery, while those who lived in Aldergrove often chose to be buried at the Aberdeen Cemetery, a small burial ground just east of the municipal border with Matsqui.

By the early 1920s it became apparent that the Murrayville Cemetery was simply too small to serve the burial needs of the township's southern half much longer. A veterans' section had been established in its northeast area, complete with a stone cenotaph in the form of a Celtic cross. The area not reserved for veterans was becoming full (though many of the plots already sold remained unoccupied).

On 13 May 1922, cemetery commissioner Robert Monahan advised council that the surveyed portion of the cemetery "was nearly all now occupied." A year later he recommended that additional land be acquired to accommodate parking. Council subsequently decided to level and lay out the unsurveyed portion of the cemetery and to explore the feasibility of acquiring more land. The Township also seems to have discovered that, although it had paid the Odd Fellows for the cemetery in 1904, the change in title had never been registered. This omission was not rectified until September 1925.

In the mid-1920s, negotiations were opened with Hugh and Charlie Haggerty, who owned land to the south. In April 1926, council made an offer of $150 per acre for two and three-quarter acres of the Haggerty brothers' land. The offer was declined, the brothers instead generously offering the land, plus a roadway, at no cost to the Township.

Like the Fort Langley Cemetery, the Murrayville Cemetery experienced the modernizing influences of the lawn cemetery movement beginning in the 1920s. These are most obvious in the area donated by the Haggerty brothers. Defined by an elliptical drive bordered by mature hardwoods, the newer section was developed entirely without vertical monuments. All the markers are low, their surfaces generally flush with the ground. When the new section was laid out, a central pathway bisected it. However, lack of space (occasioned by population growth in the City of Langley and Brookswood) ultimately resulted in this area being reclaimed for burial purposes, with the graves lying north-south rather than the traditional east-west.

The older section of the cemetery has a mixture of monument types, ranging from Alexander Murray's finely sculpted tablet and the McInnes family's obelisk to the distinctive low plaques marking the graves of veterans. Because many of the graves in this section were not occupied prior to the prohibition of vertical monuments, the older section is also home to dozens of low bronze or granite markers.

Most of the lots in the Murrayville Cemetery have now been sold, though many remain unoccupied. As a consequence, since 1966, most central and south Langley residents seeking plots but not owning space within the cemetery have elected to be buried in the Township's newest burial facility, the Langley Lawn Cemetery.

General View of Murrayville Cemetery

JOHN JACKSON
1892

John Jackson's grave appears to be the oldest in the Murrayville Cemetery. Little is known about Jackson, but he seems to have come to Langley in the early 1890s, taking up a quarter section a mile southeast of Murrayville's Five Corners. Jackson died tragically a short time later, aged 50, killed by a tree he was falling, sadly, on Christmas Day.

Jackson's stone is somewhat atypical of the 1890s, being formed from a thick, squat block of marble. Interestingly, its maker carved the letter "n" in the word "John" backwards. This suggests that an apprentice may have done part of the work. The marker bears an ominous text, one that was common on nineteenth-century markers in eastern Canada:

> Remember me as you pass by
> As you are now so once was I
> As I am now you soon shall be
> So now prepare to follow me.

ALEXANDER MURRAY
1884

Alexander Murray was the son of Langley pioneers Paul and Lucy Murray, for whom the Murrayville area was named. Murray and a friend died tragically in the Fraser River in the winter of 1884 as Murray attempted to save the other from drowning after their rowboat capsized. Murray was originally buried in the Fort Langley Cemetery, there being no other organized cemetery in Langley at the time. His remains and headstone were moved to the Murrayville Cemetery sometime after it opened in 1891, a reflection of a pioneer family's need to have the remains of their loved one close to home.

Murray's marker is an exceptionally fine example of the late-nineteenth-century stonecutter's craft. Carved from marble, the monument features an elegant floral border and inscriptions in several styles of lettering. It is virtually identical to John Beaton McLeod's 1883 monument in the Fort Langley Cemetery, both rendered by New Westminster monument maker Alexander Hamilton. Like other markers of its time, the Murray stone bears a religious text, an indication of the family's Presbyterian faith:

> All flesh is grass, and
> the goodness thereof
> is as the flower of the
> field.

MILTON FAMILY PLOT
1899 to 1906

A pedestal marks the graves of seven members of Cloverdale's Milton family. Albert Milton, the family's patriarch, was one of several Surrey residents who purchased plots when the Cloverdale Odd Fellows Lodge controlled the cemetery. Milton was a native of Elgin County, Ontario, who moved to Surrey to farm in 1881, aged 21. In 1892, he married Luetta Campbell, whose family had settled in what was then known as Clover Valley. Albert and Luetta were active in a number of community organizations, including the Surrey Fair, the Cloverdale Presbyterian Church, and the Cloverdale Opera House. The couple's farm became the site of the Surrey Co-operative, and later yet, the site of Cloverdale's principal shopping mall.

The Miltons' grey granite obelisk is embellished with a laurel leaf motif (symbolic of victory). It was probably erected in the first decade of the twentieth century, when several members of the family (Daniel, Ernest, and Edward) died. An unnamed child, simply identified at "Baby Milton," was the first to be buried, in 1899, just eleven days old. Albert Milton died in 1932; his wife followed him in 1947.

McINNES FAMILY PLOT
1899 to 1956

A grey granite tombstone in the form of a gabled obelisk, a style very much in vogue in the early 1900s, marks the graves of Murrayville pioneers Roderick ("Rod") and Isabella McInnes. The couple arrived in Langley from Ontario in 1887, settling on a quarter section at the corner of 40th Avenue and 224th Street. Rod and Isabella had ten children, many of whom are commemorated on the family monument. Rod McInnes and his wife were very active in the life of their church, Sharon Presbyterian, at Murrayville's Five Corners. Rod served as an elder from 1892 until his death in 1899. Tradition states that the lumber for the church was milled from logs felled on the McInnes property.

The McInnes monument features several sandblasted decorative motifs: ivy, a bundle of wheat, and a fleur-de-lis. The ivy is symbolic of immortality; the sheaf of wheat refers to the body of Christ; the fleur-de-lis may represent ardour.

NEIL and CHRISTINE BEATON
1901 & 1904

Gable-topped obelisks were common cemetery monuments in the first two decades of the twentieth century. The Beatons' stone was rendered from grey granite, a material that was popular for tombstones in the early 1900s. Similar stones in the cemetery were made from red granite or grey-white marble. The Beaton monument incorporates a sandblasted thistle, a symbol of Neil's Scottish origins. The monument sits on a raised stone base into which the name "Beaton" is carved in raised relief.

Surrey resident Neil Beaton was a member of the Odd Fellows Lodge who died at the age of 92. His wife predeceased him, aged 82.

LIVINGSTONE FAMILY PLOT
1903 to 1924

Murrayville residents James and Catherine Livingstone and their family probably settled in Langley in the early 1890s, taking up five quarter sections along 232nd Street (initially known as Livingstone Road) between 1891 and 1901. John died in 1903 and was one of Murrayville's few early settlers who were borne from Sharon Presbyterian Church in a horse-drawn hearse, a general store delivery wagon being the more usual conveyance. James and Catherine's son John was buried in the family plot in 1912. John's mother followed him in 1921. Another son, Robert, was buried in 1924.

Other members of the family are also buried in the plot, which is marked by a massive, roughly cut block of grey granite, with raised lead lettering. The stone, which is typical of those erected in the 1920s, was probably not installed until after Catherine's death.

PAUL and LUCY (BRUCE) MURRAY
1904 & 1911

Paul and Lucy Murray and several of their adult children came to Langley from Ontario in the mid-1870s, taking up several quarter sections near the corner of 216th Street and 48th Avenue (then part of the New Westminster and Yale Wagon Road). As they were the earliest settlers in the area, it was only natural that their name should become associated with the community. Originally known as Murrays' Corners, the vibrant community that emerged at the Five Corners came in time to be known as Murrayville. During their time in Langley, members of the family were involved in pursuits ranging from farming to construction to hotel keeping, and were active supporters of Sharon Presbyterian Church.

The Murrays' stone, which also commemorates two of their sons and a daughter, clearly illustrates how tastes in cemetery monuments had changed in the twenty years since their son Alexander's death. By the early 1900s, obelisk-like monuments had largely supplanted the tablets that had been popular throughout the 1800s. Further, the choice of materials had also changed. Gleaming white marble was often replaced by granite, in the more earthy tones of grey, black, or red. Gone too were the long Biblical texts that had testified to the faith of the deceased and their families. Paul and Lucy's stone simply records their names and dates of birth and death. It also serves to mark the burials of many people, whereas in previous years, separate stones – one for each person – would likely have been required.

JOHNSTON and MARGARET NELSON
1907

The Nelsons' impressive monument is quite unlike any other in Langley's cemeteries. Hewn from red granite and subsequently polished smooth, the marker consists of a sphere supported by a pedestal. The creation of the sphere, which is perfectly round, must have been a considerable challenge to its maker. In the symbolism of the time, the sphere was intended to represent eternity, in that it has no beginning and no end.

Johnston and Margaret Nelson were apparently the second family to settle in Murrayville, arriving from Orillia, Ontario, in the winter of 1880. Their quarter section was located on either side of the Old Yale Road, about half a mile east of the Five Corners. Johnston Nelson operated Langley's first steam-powered sawmill and supplied lumber for the construction of Sharon Presbyterian Church. He also helped to design the church, while he and his sons helped to build it. Johnston Nelson died on 10 January 1907, aged 76. His grief-stricken wife, aged 66, followed him just seven days later.

THOMAS and MARY (ROBERTSON) SHANNON
1909 & 1931

Thomas and Mary Shannon were early settlers in Surrey's Cloverdale area. Thomas was very active in civic affairs, serving as Surrey's first warden (mayor). He was a member of the Cloverdale Odd Fellows Lodge, so it was only natural for him to purchase a plot for his family in the organization's cemetery at Murrayville. Other Surrey families – the Bothwells, Beatons, Miltons, and Murphys – also had connections with the lodge, so they too were buried in Murrayville. Thomas predeceased Mary by twenty-two years. The couple had five children including a daughter, Mary Jane, who wrote fiction and taught throughout the province. She was recognized when the Surrey School District named a school in her honour.

Thomas's grave likely remained unmarked until after Mary's death, for their monument was clearly manufactured in the 1930s. It is formed from roughly hewn grey granite, and the stone's inscription is in applied, raised lead letters, a practice common in the 1930s. The stone also features carved acanthus leaves, symbols of peace or the heavenly garden. Other members of the Shannon family lie nearby.

GEORGE and MARGARET PORTER
1921 & 1911

The Porter name has been virtually synonymous with Murrayville for over a century. The family's founders, George and Margaret, came to the area from Gore Bay, Ontario, in the early 1890s, taking up a homestead about 2.5 kilometres east of Murrayville's Five Corners, on what was then the New Westminster and Yale Wagon Road. The property became the site of the Porter family farm and blacksmith shop, and home to the couple's six children. One son, Philip Young Porter (generally known as "P.Y.") purchased the Murrayville general store in 1917. The property has remained in the family ever since. P.Y.'s son, Eldie, operated the store after his father's retirement, his roadside displays of lawn mowers becoming a local legend. The store, which was rebuilt in 1939-40, remains a focal point in the life of the community, currently operating as a popular local coffee shop.

George Porter purchased his family plot, which contained space for nine graves, prior to the cemetery's sale to the Township in 1904. The family's monument is a polished grey granite screen embellished with sandblasted classical motifs.

ISAMU SUGAYA and CHIYOKO OIKAWA
1912 & 1922

Two stones mark the graves of Japanese Canadians in the older part of the cemetery. Inscribed entirely in Japanese, one denotes the grave of Isamu Sugaya. Isamu was the third son of Harujiro Sugaya. He was born in Fujyu village in Katori County, in Japan's Chiba Prefecture. The stone states that he died on 30 November during the first year of the Taisho Period, that is, in 1912.

The stone immediately to the north is that of Chiyoko Oikawa, who was a native of Yonekawa village in Kanaki County in the Miyagi Prefecture. Chiyoko was the second daughter of Shonosuke Oikawa and died on 2 September in the eleventh year of the Taisho Period (1922). The Sugayas and Oikawas were likely connected with one of the several sawmills that operated in the Murrayville area in the early 1900s. The Murray & McAdam and the Galbraith sawmills both apparently employed multiracial labour.

The two stones, which were initially installed in an erect position, closely resemble those that would have been erected in Japan at the same time, noting the regnal year of the emperor, rather than the western year.

WILLIAM and GRACE (SMITH) McDONALD
1918 & 1934

Scots-born William McDonald came to British Columbia from the Ottawa Valley with his brother Jim, in the 1880s. The two brothers were lumbermen, and on arriving in Langley, they found work in the Baumgartner Sawmill in Murrayville. In 1908, the pair opened their own sawmill on what later became 48th Avenue, on the plateau east of Murrayville's Five Corners. William served as the mill's sawyer, Jim as its engineer, and William's wife, the former Grace Smith, cooked for the mill's fourteen resident employees. William McDonald died in 1918, having lost his brother Jim, and his son Gordon, in the First World War. Grace followed him to the grave in 1934. The couple's youngest son, George, a motorcycle policeman, is the only other member of the family known to be buried in the plot. He was killed in an automobile accident in 1927.

The McDonald monument is a massive grey granite screen similar in design and scale to the Porter and Deans family monuments that stand nearby.

DANIEL McINNES
1920

Daniel McInnes was one of the fourteen children of Murrayville pioneers Rod and Isabella McInnes. Born in Bruce County, Ontario, in 1886, Daniel travelled west with his parents and eight surviving siblings when still an infant, in 1887. Orphaned at the age of 14, Daniel appears to have been raised by his elder brothers and sisters. Daniel enlisted in the Canadian Expeditionary Force in September 1914, just five weeks after the declaration of war. Assigned to the 7th Infantry Battalion, Daniel was a somewhat rebellious soldier who was plagued by periods of ill health. He was ultimately diagnosed with tuberculosis and invalided to Canada. He died of the disease in the provincial hospital at Tranquille on 30 May 1920.

Daniel's was the second burial of a returned soldier in the Murrayville Cemetery, occurring just days after the dedication of the cenotaph there. Although his family could have had his remains interred in what was to become the veterans' section of the cemetery, they chose instead to bury him near the graves of his parents. His monument, which is now laid flat, follows the specifications laid out by the Commonwealth War Graves Commission, bearing his name, rank, and serial number as well as the name of the unit in which he served.

BARBARA DEANS
1923

Albert and Barbara Deans were prominent residents of Murrayville in the early 1900s. Their home was on the Old Yale Road, northwest of the Five Corners, on a quarter section originally owned by William Ramage, the first commissioner of the Murrayville Cemetery. Albert was at various times a local magistrate and a school trustee. The couple hosted many church picnics on an area of their property north of 48th Avenue commonly known as "Deans Grove." Barbara Deans died in 1923 at the age of 72. Her husband subsequently moved to California where he remarried and eventually died.

Barbara's monument is a massive, polished grey granite block with sandblasted leaf and garland decoration. It is virtually identical to the Porter family monument, which dates from 1921.

RONNIE BERRY
1925

Two unrelated Berry families have been prominent in the history of the Murrayville area. John Walter Berry, who operated the general store at Murrayville's Five Corners, and who also started a sizeable dairy farm, was the patriarch of the first, arriving in Langley in 1897. Harry Berry and his brother Owen headed the other Berry family. Harry operated a general store at the corner of the Old Yale Road and 232nd Street and later, a larger one at the corner of the Fraser Highway and 232nd Street. Owen's wife Eva operated a maternity hospital on 56th Avenue from 1924 to 1948. Owen and Eva's son Ronnie died in 1925 aged just three and one-half. As his death was never registered, his monument may be the only record of his ever having existed.

Ronnie's stone, a plain, small marble tablet, documents the belief of his survivors that he was "Budded on earth to bloom in Heaven."

THOROLD F. WILLIAMS
1926

A small monument marks the grave of young Thorold Frank Williams, who died in 1926 two weeks shy of his 5th birthday. Like many children at the time, Thorold fell victim to measles, a childhood disease that is now far less dangerous. Thorold is buried next to his father, Capt. Francis Williams, owner of Langley Greenhouses Ltd. from 1919 to 1958.

In keeping with attempts in the early twentieth century to downplay the finality of death, the inscription on Thorold's stone describes the deceased as one who "fell asleep." The stone itself is a short marble tablet. It bears a short, sentimental text:

> No sordidness of life can stain
> No weight of woe can crush
> This little child of mine.

RICHMOND ARCHIBALD and HELEN (McLUCKIE) PAYNE
1957 & 1931

Richmond Archibald ("Archie") Payne was one of Langley's most prominent citizens for a full half-century. Payne was born in the Scottish border town of Langholm in 1882 and immigrated to Canada just after the turn of the century. Arriving in Langley in 1902, Payne followed a number of pursuits, working as municipal licence collector until 1916, when he enlisted in the Canadian Expeditionary Force. Prior to enlisting, Payne had helped to organize the Langley Volunteers, a unit of men ultimately designated as a squadron in the 31st B.C. Horse. Payne's service overseas earned him the Military Cross and he returned to Langley to take up the position of municipal clerk. After the outbreak of the Second World War, Payne left Langley to serve in the Canadian forces once again, rising to the rank of major. On his return to Langley, Payne opened a highly successful real estate and insurance business. He also served as a local lay magistrate. Upon his death in 1957, Payne was eulogized as one of Langley's most community-minded citizens. He had been named a Freeman of the City of Langley just months before his death.

Archie Payne's monument also marks the grave of his wife, Helen, who died prematurely in 1931, aged 41. The Paynes' monument is a plain black plaque bearing the inscription "Forever with the Lord," a testament to the couple's Presbyterian faith, and a simple thistle decoration, a reflection of the Paynes' Scottish origins.

YUZO and HARU SAKAMOTO
1954 & 1937

The Sakamoto monument is a reminder of the once large, but now largely forgotten Japanese Canadian population that lived in Langley between the two world wars. During this period, a number of Japanese Canadian families created successful berry farms on what had previously been considered marginal land in a number of upland areas, including West Langley, Fern Ridge, and Coghlan. The Sakamotos lived in the area prior to being interned along with all other Japanese Canadians on the West Coast after the bombing of Pearl Harbour in 1941.

The Sakamoto monument is a low, grey granite screen. Its design is similar to the nearby monument of the Takaoka family, another Japanese-Canadian family who also once lived in the area. The Sakamoto and Takaoka family plots are surrounded by the graves of their European neighbours, since racial segregation was never a practice in any of Langley's municipal cemeteries.

JOHN WALTER and LYDIA (BOWMAN) BERRY
1943 & 1948

John Walter Berry, his wife Lydia, and their first two children arrived in Murrayville from Ontario in 1897. "Jack" Berry, as he was commonly known, had taught school in the Kitchener-Waterloo area, where he met his future wife, a member of the local Mennonite community. The couple's move to Langley was prompted by Berry's long-time friend, David Moss Coulter, who had convinced him to partner in the purchase of two general stores, one in Murrayville, the other in Fort Langley. The Berrys operated the Murrayville store for several years; they then turned their attention to farming, operating the Belmont Dairy Farm for over forty years. Jack Berry was also active in the community, serving as municipal clerk, chair of the school board, and president of the Fraser Valley Milk Producers' Association. He also served a term as Member of the Legislative Assembly for the constituency of Delta, a large riding, that then encompassed much of the Lower Fraser Valley.

The Berrys' stone is located in the newest section of the Murrayville Cemetery. Like most of those that surround it, the monument is a simple black stone plaque, laid flush with the level of the lawn.

JAMES HUGH MONAHAN
1954

The Monahan family is among Murrayville's earliest, being preceded only by the Nelsons and the Murrays. Simon and Margaret Monahan were from Ontario and took up property on the Old Yale Road in 1882. The couple had two sons, one of whom, James ("Jim"), joined the Canadian Siberian Expeditionary Force during the First World War. Jim served in the 260th Battalion, a unit raised to fight the Bolshevists who had seized power in Russia in 1917. After hostilities in Siberia had ended, Jim returned to Langley where he worked as a logger and sawmill employee. Jim died in 1954 at the age of 62.

Though not located in the veterans' section of the cemetery, James Monahan's flush-mounted stone plaque is a "lawn cemetery" version of the vertical tablets that were used on veterans' graves earlier in the century.

HUGH and MARTHA (GREER) HALLACK
1954 & 1931

The Hallack monument is a charming example of an early response to the requirements of the lawn cemetery movement. The stone is low but not flush to the ground. It is rendered from white marble in the form of an open Bible. A cross marks the exposed page. One page incorporates Hugh Hallack's particulars (1874-1954), the other his wife Martha's (1872-1931). The couple's young daughter, Edna Tressa, died in 1914, three months shy of her third birthday. She is buried near her parents in an unmarked grave.

Hugh Hallack was born in Michigan and had farmed in Langley's Milner area for forty years prior to his death. Martha was born in Ontario. As was common in the mid-twentieth century, the text on the couple's stone is simple in the extreme, reading simply "At Rest."

DAVID WILLIAM and SARAH JANE (BEST) POPPY
1957 & 1960

David William Poppy was one of early Langley's most distinguished and respected residents. Poppy came to British Columbia in 1884. As this was prior to the completion of the Canadian Pacific Railway, Poppy had to walk from Banff to Spence's Bridge. On reaching Langley, he acquired a quarter section at the Old Yale Road and 248th Street and began life as a farmer. Poppy soon became involved in the life of the community and ultimately served as a school trustee, councillor, and reeve. At one point during the First World War, when so many local men were overseas, he simultaneously filled the positions of clerk, treasurer, tax collector, and assessor.

Poppy was Langley's longest-serving reeve, holding the position for nineteen years. For a number of years, he also served as a local magistrate. When he died in 1957, the *Langley Advance* described him as "the patriarch of local municipal government." Poppy and his wife, Sarah, who died in 1960, shared fifty-two years of married life. The remains of several of the Poppys' children lie nearby, including those of David William ("Bill") Poppy (1906-2004), whose involvement in the life of the community, including fifteen years serving as reeve, rivalled that of his father.

David and Sarah Poppy are remembered with a polished black granite plaque that acknowledges a "life's work well done."

CAPTAIN FRANCIS WILLIAMS, M.C.
1958

Returned soldier Capt. Francis Surridge Williams arrived in Langley Prairie in 1919, when he and his associates, Col. Victor Spencer and Col. Frank Ross, purchased the Timms Market Gardens. The partners' new enterprise was a large greenhouse operation located on the site of what later became the Langley Mall. For the next four decades, Williams, portrayed by the local press as a "forthright" figure, cultivated a variety of flowers for distribution to markets throughout western North America. When he died in 1958, his funeral featured what the *Langley Advance* described as "one of the most tremendous displays of floral tributes ever shown," which was appropriate enough, given the nature of his business activities.

Williams's red stone monument is of rather modest proportions, considering the status he enjoyed in life. Interestingly, its installation failed to comply with the cemetery bylaw of the day, which forbade the erection of vertical monuments in any of the Township's cemeteries. This exception to the rules was perhaps tolerated given Williams's importance in the life of the community.

JULIA E. F. (LAMB) MULLIGAN
1994

The Mulligan family name is well known in Langley, its various members having distinguished themselves in a range of endeavours for over fifty years. The family's patriarch, Frank Mulligan, who had previously worked as a farmer, opened a trucking company in Langley Prairie in 1947, assisted by his sons, Myles, Wallace, and Warren. The three young men went on to distinguish themselves in business and the public service, while a fourth son, Maurice, became the City of Langley's first solicitor, and ultimately, a Provincial Court judge. Frank's wife, Julia, was no less distinguished, working as a counsellor and as a volunteer with the local Women's Institute and Langley Prairie's United Church.

Julia Mulligan's monument, a black stone plaque, bears inscriptions reflecting her dual roles, firstly as a much cherished parent ("Our Beloved Mother"), and secondly, as one whose efforts benefited people throughout the community ("Her Memory Will Gladden the Darkest Day").

VETERANS' SECTION

Like the Fort Langley Cemetery, the Murrayville Cemetery also contains a section reserved for the burials of veterans. Men who died overseas were buried near where they had died, among their comrades. Provided by the Commonwealth War Graves Commission, all their stones were identical in design, regardless of rank. Unable to visit loved ones' graves abroad, grieving relatives occasionally remembered their fallen relatives on their own stones in Canada. The Keet family monument in the Murrayville Cemetery is one such stone. It commemorates Robert and Beatrice Keet as well as their son Sgt. James Keet who was killed in action in Italy in 1944.

A grey granite cenotaph, in the form of a Celtic cross, dominates the veterans' section, recording the names of men from Langley who died in the two world wars. The veterans' section went unused for a number of years after the installation of the cenotaph, deceased soldiers instead being buried in other areas of the cemetery. While the Fort Langley veterans' section contains burials dating from the early 1920s, the first marked burial in the veterans' section at Murrayville was that of Coghlan resident L/Corp. Herbert A. Cannell who died in 1941 at Esquimalt, while serving with the Canadian Scottish Regiment. The first burial of a veteran elsewhere in the cemetery was that of Pte. Stanley Jefferson, who died of lung disease worsened by the war, in 1920.

EDWARD TADEUSZ OLEJNIK
1972

Capt. Edward Olejnik's monument in the Murrayville Cemetery's veterans' section is a reminder of the diversity of those who fought on the Allied side during the Second World War. Despite being defeated by the Germans in a blitzkrieg campaign early in the war, the Poles determined to rid themselves of the invaders. Many of them found their way to Britain, where they regrouped and planned the liberation of their homeland. Arriving in British Columbia in 1948 with his wife and family, Capt. Olejnik, a civil engineer who had served in the 1st Polish Armoured Division, surveyed areas such as Williams Park. He died at the family home on Coghlan Road in 1972 and was laid to rest among his Canadian and British comrades in arms.

Like markers commemorating Canadian veterans, Captain Olejnik's black granite, flush-mounted plaque records his unit and the dates and places of his birth and death. The monument also features an eagle, the heraldic symbol of his Polish homeland.

St. Alban's Anglican Churchyard

Located on the east side of 216th Street north of 61st Avenue, St. Alban's Anglican Churchyard is among the smallest of Langley's cemeteries. This small area encompasses just two graves and is all that remains of a larger property once owned by the Anglican Church in Langley's Milner district.

Milner's Church of St. Alban the Martyr was consecrated on 1 June 1890. A vicarage, still standing, was built across the street. The church was the only Anglican place of worship in Langley until the construction of St. George's Anglican Church in Fort Langley in 1900.

In the late nineteenth century, rural Anglican churches commonly had their own burial grounds. Examples abound on southern Vancouver Island and in the Gulf Islands, areas of the province favoured by English settlers. The practice was less common on the mainland, where Anglicans tended to bury their dead in municipally operated interdenominational cemeteries rather than in churchyards. In the Fraser Valley, three notable exceptions are found in Surrey (Christ Church, at Surrey Centre; St. Helen's, at South Westminster; and St. Oswald's, at Port Kells).

St. Alban's remained in use until 1925. It was subsequently dismantled and moved to Langley's Otter district (near the corner of 248th Street and the Fraser Highway) where it was reassembled in

1926. Its churchyard saw just two burials. The first was probably that of one of the children of Thomas and Ellen Culbert, formerly of Ontario. The second burial is that of Ellen, who died in 1894. A well-preserved marble tablet marks Ellen's grave. The stone features a relief portraying clasped hands, notes Mrs. Culbert's dates (1844-1894), and includes a sentimental text:

> We shall meet again sweet mother
> In a brighter clime than this
> Where the anguish of this
> world of ours
> Is lost in endless bliss.

A wooden cross, installed by members of St. Andrew's Anglican Church, marks the unidentified burial. Interestingly, both markers, and presumably both burials, face the west, contrary to traditional Anglican practice. The church may have felt it more important to acknowledge the presence of the road than the niceties of past practice.

Langley eventually became home to two additional Anglican congregations. A church dedicated to St. Dunstan, was built in Aldergrove in 1911, while another, named for St. Andrew, was opened in Langley Prairie in 1922. The congregation of the latter church eventually developed a memorial garden for the scattering of cremated remains. After its building burned in 1979, the soil from the garden was moved to the grounds of the relocated and rebuilt church.

McQuilken Burial

THE McQuilken burial is one of the few known instances of a single burial having been made on an isolated farmstead in Langley. Located on the west side of 232nd Street a half-mile north of 0 Avenue, the grave in question is that of Ann McQuilken, an aunt of nineteenth-century settler John Alexander Cameron.

Ann McQuilken was born in Scotland in 1824. She joined her nephew, his wife, and their family of six when they took up three quarter sections in the south Langley area in 1887. McQuilken was alive at the time of the 1891 census but appears to have died sometime around the turn of the century. Tradition states that prior to her death she expressed a wish to be buried on the Cameron property under her favourite tree, overlooking a creek.

Cameron and his family honoured her request and marked her burial site with a picket fence enclosure that has long since rotted away. No stone appears to have been erected on her grave, although there may once have been a wooden marker. Although its general location has been determined and recorded, the exact location of McQuilken's grave has long since been forgotten.

The 8th Avenue Burials

A site on the north side of 8th Avenue, just west of 256th Street, is thought to contain the remains of two girls, one Native, the other of European descent. The sole record of the burials is an oral one, having been passed from one property owner to the next as the site changed hands.

The site of the burials is a small knoll, now covered with mature conifers, with what must once have been a wonderful view of Mount Baker to the southeast. The burials are said to have been made sometime before the turn of the century.

The property was initially owned by Lars Larsen Broe, who, with his brothers Andrew and John, ran a hop growing and curing operation on three quarter sections in the area in the 1890s. The 1891 census records Lars as living on the property with his wife Ellen and their daughter Lena, then three years old. Though the grave may be Lena's, there is no way to be certain of this. The identity of the Native child has not been preserved, though she may have been a member of the Matsqui First Nation, which owns a reserve, now leased as a mobile home park, two miles to the east.

Patricia Lutheran Churchyard

PATRICIA is an old community just north of the Aldergrove border crossing on either side of 264th Street. In addition to the border crossing, the community at one time boasted a post office (from 1912 to 1917), a school, a community hall, and a Lutheran church. At the turn of the century, the area's population was of mixed origins and included a modest number of Scandinavian families, thus explaining the need for a Lutheran place of worship.

The church appears to have been built in the early 1900s and was last used about 1921. It was then sold to Walter and Ada Wilson and converted to a private residence. Three people are buried in the churchyard, tradition identifying them only as a mother and two children. It is thought that they died, possibly of smallpox or during a house fire, sometime shortly after the church was built. Their names are unknown, but they may have been members of one of the northern and central European families living in the area at the time: the Hansens, Heines, Hoffmans, Larsons, Swansons, and Olsons.

That they were buried next to the church may be explained in a number of ways. Their survivors may have wished to bury them close to home, in sanctified ground, rather than in a secular cemetery in distant Aberdeen. (The Aberdeen cemetery is east of Aldergrove, across the Abbotsford border, on the

Former Lutheran Church, Patricia

north side of the Fraser Highway.) Alternatively, if the three did die of smallpox, a quarantine may have been imposed, and there may have been a need to reduce the possibility of contagion by burying the deceased quickly, in the most convenient spot.

The 200th Street Burial

OF all the burial sites in Langley, the 200th Street burial is perhaps the most mysterious. Long-time residents of the Fern Ridge area recall a grave being located under a cherry tree on the west side of 200th Street south of 21st Avenue, about 75 feet from the road. As the cherry tree has long since vanished, there is no way to determine the exact location of the grave with any accuracy.

David Wix owned the property in question in 1908, but the identity of earlier owners has not been determined. The property is across 200th Street from a quarter section originally owned by Jason Samuel Lewis. Lewis was related by marriage to the Walworth family, who lived just to the south. The grave could be that of a member of Lewis's family, perhaps felled by the same smallpox epidemic that hit the Walworth family in 1888.

Langley Lawn Cemetery

THE Langley Lawn Cemetery is the Township's newest burial ground and incorporates ideas about cemetery design and management that first came to the fore in the 1920s. Prior to that time, cemeteries had followed traditions set in the nineteenth century. Vertical monuments proliferated and fences, curbs, or plantings further defined the individuality of each grave. By the 1920s, however, new attitudes toward cemeteries and the commemoration of the dead decreed that burial places should be less "obtrusive" and that their design should maximize the number of plots available while minimizing the costs of maintenance. This approach continued to be popular throughout the twentieth century, especially with municipally operated cemeteries.

By the late 1950s council became increasing aware that Langley was about to face a burial crisis. While a large number of plots remained unsold in the Fort Langley Cemetery, the Murrayville Cemetery – the Township's only other active burial ground – was on the verge of being sold out. Provincial legislation did not permit the resale of unused plots, and many central and south Langley residents preferred not to be buried in far-off Fort Langley.

In 1959, council decided to acquire land for a new cemetery. A Cemetery Advisory Committee was established under the chairmanship of Ben Greer to advise on possible sites. The location initially selected for the proposed new cemetery was in Sperling, at 240th Street and 72nd Avenue. The site was eventually rejected, several vocal residents of the area having opposed it on the grounds that children at the nearby school might be traumatized were they to witness a funeral taking place. The committee looked for alternative sites throughout the township. The site ultimately chosen, on 208th Street south of 44th Avenue, was then far away from any of Langley's urban areas. Councillor Eric Flowerdew led the campaign to acquire the land and, as chairman of the Cemetery Advisory Committee, oversaw much of its early development. Construction, however, was delayed by council's decision in 1962 to increase the capacity of the Murrayville Cemetery by 316 graves. This was accomplished by allowing burials under the trees and by moving the roadway against the cemetery's fence.

The development of the new cemetery eventually went ahead, a total of fourteen acres having been acquired with the intent of developing the new facility in phases. The cemetery was from the outset divided into five sections, and the first to be developed had a capacity of 2,400 plots. It took three years to develop the site to meet the stringent regulations of the Province's Public Utilities Commission. A water supply had to be procured from the City of Langley and a new bylaw to govern the cemetery's operation had to be approved by the commission. The bylaw went back and forth between the Township and Victoria for five frustrating months before it was finally approved, delaying the opening of the cemetery substantially. In accordance with the bylaw, new rates

Memorial to Unknown Babies

were set for burials in all the Township's cemeteries: $55 for residents and $70 for non-residents, with an extra fee of $10 being levied for burials on statutory holidays, weekends, or after 4:30 p.m.

By September 1966, the new bylaw was approved and the Township proceeded to open the new cemetery. The inaugural ceremonies on 17 September featured a short dedicatory service by the Langley Ministerial Association followed by an official opening by Councillor Ralph Barichello. Due to inclement weather, the service and opening took place in the cemetery's less than elegant concrete block tool shed, amid a stock of hand tools, overalls, and hard hats.

The cemetery's first burial took place just over a month later, when nine-year-old Brian Dean Nybeck was laid to rest. Two burials occurred the following day: Alfred Erik Vickman, aged 68, and Richard Allen Ladd, aged less than two months. Since that time the Langley Lawn Cemetery has accommodated over 3,000 additional burials. By the end of 1997 very few unsold plots remained, resulting in an expansion of the cemetery to the west beginning early in 1998. Other recent developments have included the construction of stone-faced columbaria in a grove of conifers on the cemetery's eastern side, in recognition of public interest in creative alternatives for the deposition of cremated remains. A memorial garden has also been created, for the unmarked deposition of cremated remains. The garden may be unique, insofar as it contains an area dedicated to the memory of babies who died while very young.

The Langley Lawn Cemetery differs from the two other municipally operated cemeteries in the township in a number of ways. The first and most obvious difference lies in its lack of vertical monuments, the cemetery having been opened several decades after they were prohibited. While a few jurisdictions now permit the installation of vertical monuments, Langley has not yet changed its policies. The Langley Lawn Cemetery also lacks the family plots so apparent in the township's older cemeteries. Although a husband and wife might be buried together in the Langley Lawn Cemetery (two adjacent graves being the maximum allowable purchase under the Township's cemetery regulations), there is less likelihood of other family members being buried adjacent to them (unless the remains buried are cremated remains, which occupy less space and can be clustered atop an inhumation).

A New Approach to Monument Design

Because all the burials in the Langley Lawn Cemetery date from 1966 or later, most of the sentiments expressed on the monuments represent those of the second half of the twentieth century and thus differ from many of those found in the Fort Langley or Murrayville cemeteries. Like many monuments dating from the 1930s, 1940s, and 1950s, the monuments of the 1960s and 1970s often record only the name of the deceased and his or her years of birth and death. Many monuments from this period bear little or no embellishment, save perhaps, for a modest floral design. Epitaphs are few and brief. Furthermore, during these two decades, monument designs appear to have been endlessly repeated, drawing their inspiration from what must have been the thinnest of printed catalogues. Such monuments may be as revealing for what they don't say as for what they do say. Was this a period of increasing secularism or diminished sentimentality, or was it simply an era when monument makers lost all sense of imagination? Perhaps during this period people's attitudes toward death were more ambiguous than in the early twentieth century. Whatever social or religious forces were at work, the cemetery landscape of the mid-twentieth century was often bleak,

with few monuments expressing the individuality of those they commemorated.

By the early 1980s, monument design began to change, not just in Langley, but throughout the province. Though still restricted to a horizontal format, new technologies and, perhaps, changes in how society was dealing with death led to greater individual expression in cemetery monuments. In Langley, this new generation of monuments is most easily viewed at the Langley Lawn Cemetery (being the largest and newest of Langley's three active cemeteries), but examples can also be seen in the Fort Langley and Murrayville cemeteries.

A walk through the Langley Lawn Cemetery is best begun in the east, where the earliest graves are clustered. The area is also home to the cemetery's stone-faced columbaria, installed in 1998, as well as to a number of in-ground cremation plots. Inhumations from the 1960s and 1970s lie slightly to the west, with those from subsequent decades increasing in number as one walks toward the west. As noted above, the earliest monuments in the cemetery are often quite spartan, while those from later decades are generally richer, in both a textual and a graphic sense.

If they bear any epitaphs at all, the earliest monuments in the cemetery repeat the hackneyed lines found on thousands of memorials dating from the mid-twentieth century and earlier. "In Loving Memory," "At Rest," "Gone But Not Forgotten," or "Rest in Peace" are common among their texts. Some epitaphs found in the cemetery have endured for over a century, such as the one on a memorial to a nine-day-old baby that reads, "Budded on Earth to Bloom in Heaven."

More recent epitaphs, however, are often more innovative than these earlier examples. There is the grave of a former newspaper editor who died in 1981. His bronze monument records an appropriate verse, which counsels in part,

Think again before you utter
Words that give another pain …

There are also briefer epitaphs, such as one in honour of a ten-year-old girl that reads simply "Specially Picked," suggesting that a higher power had called the deceased to immortality. A former mayor is remembered with the inscription "Life's Work Well Done," a tribute to his many years of public service. Some epitaphs evoke the twin emotions of love and loss, such as one on the monument of a fifteen-year-old teen:

Loved by all who knew him
Missed by all who loved him.

Abiding love is equally expressed in shorter phrases, such as the simple "We Love You" and "Never Will Your Memory Fade." Familial ties come through in epitaphs that identify the deceased as "Our Beloved Son," "Forever in Our Hearts," a "Loving Husband, Father, and Papa," "Dearest Mom," and the more direct "We Love You." While virtually all such messages are inscribed in English, there is one that somehow seems more poetic, if only because it is written in Italian: "Con Amore in Memoria Di Nostro Figlio e Fratello" ("in loving memory of our son and brother").

Langley has often been identified as a "community of faith." With dozens of church congregations in the area, many of them evangelical, one would expect local cemetery monuments to reflect the central tenets of Christianity, including faith in the Resurrection. Not surprisingly, some of the cemetery's recent monuments feature inscriptions such as "Rejoice in My Going Home to Meet My Lord," "God's Gift Is Life Eternal," "Death Has Been Swallowed Up in Victory," "Safe in the Arms of Jesus," and "Waiting for the Resurrection."

There are also phrases that are less overtly Christian, but which nonetheless suggest faith in some sort of continued existence after death. "To Everything There Is a Season," "May We Walk Hand in Hand into Eternity," "He Heard the Muse of the Spheres," "Til We Meet Again," and "Until the Morning Comes" are typical of such sentiments.

Even more interesting, perhaps, are those epitaphs that defy convention, allowing the cemetery to become the site of irreverence and even humour. The words "Gone Fishing," often coupled with the image of a fly-fisherman playing a wily trout or steelhead, suggest an afterlife spent not on billowy clouds in the sky, but rather in some pristine wilderness of infinite extent. There is the epitaph of a seventy-year-old man, that reads "Closed for the Duration." The grave of a couple who loved music proclaims their mutual passion as a metaphor for life: "No Drum Went Dead." The words on the stone of a sixty-two-year-old woman admonish us for mourning and instead command that we "Live, Laugh, and Love." There are also a few informal messages, such as the very much to the point "Missing You, Bud" and "See You in Heaven." A few inscriptions are even more colloquial, such as the message sent to a young truck driver from his grieving widow: "Keep on Truckin' Darling!"

In comparison with their late-nineteenth-century predecessors, most of the inscriptions in the cemetery are noticeably brief. Lack of space on a small flush-mounted stone may preclude extensive poetry or prose, but the brevity of most inscriptions may also be due to tradition. The years in which the lawn cemetery was created were a time of decreased sentimentality, and the norms that were set for memorials then remained strong fifty to seventy-five years later. It is a rare monument indeed that displays an epitaph more than two lines long. The stone memorial to an eighteen-year-old youth who died in 1979 is a rare exception, repeating Mary Frye's 1932 pantheistic verse "Do Not Stand at My Grave and Weep" in its fourteen-line entirety:

> Do not stand at my grave and weep,
> I am not there, I do not sleep.
>
> I am a thousand winds that blow.
> I am the diamond glint on snow.
> I am the sunlight on ripened grain.
> I am the gentle autumn rain.
>
> When you wake in the morning hush,
> I am the swift, uplifting rush
> Of quiet birds in circling flight.
> I am the soft starlight at night.
>
> Do not stand at my grave and weep.
> I am not there, I do not sleep.
> Do not stand at my grave and cry.
> I am not there, I did not die!

Many of the epitaphs of the late twentieth and early twenty-first centuries would surprise, and even shock, members of earlier generations. The motifs on recent monuments would doubtless elicit similar responses. Were they able to speak, long-dead visitors would likely comment on the lack of true two-dimensional motifs and the utter absence of three-dimensional designs. The restrictions of the flush-mounted plaque restrict the former and prohibit the latter, but modern technologies permit motifs of which earlier generations could only dream.

Gone are the pointing fingers, clasped hands, doves, urns, and willow trees of a century ago, the symbols of a highly sentimental society. These began

to be swept aside by the lawn-park cemetery movement; their last vestiges being obliterated by the advent of the lawn cemetery after the First World War. Monuments remained bereft of significant decoration for the next several decades. Even the earliest monuments in the Langley Lawn Cemetery bear little in the way of ornament. Beginning in the late 1960s, however, decoration began to reappear, first with a limited number of stock motifs and later with customized designs reflecting distinctly individual needs and tastes. By the turn of the millennium, consumers had access to a seemingly unlimited range of designs, both sacred and profane.

Christian motifs abound in the cemetery, whether incised or sandblasted into stone or cast in relief in bronze. The cemetery's oldest monument records the name and dates of a deceased child within the etched pages of an open Bible, an image originally meant to represent both revelation and salvation. Other memorials from the same period depict

Albrecht Dürer's *Praying Hands*, an image that continues to be used into the present. Originally rendered in the fifteenth century as a drawing on paper, Dürer's image has been endlessly rendered in both stone and bronze, and is often found on stones marking the graves of Roman Catholics. Rosaries are also common on the graves of Roman Catholics. A few stones bear the image of the Sacred Heart. Some monuments incorporate illustrations of stalks of wheat, a funerary symbol often favoured by Mennonites, the wheat representing the Resurrection, the Divine Harvest, the Lord's Supper, and fertility. Other Christian symbols, many of them relating to the Resurrection, include the image of Christ in Glory, his hands upraised in blessing, as well as the image of the crucified Christ. Latin crosses abound. Eastern crosses are also in evidence, their topmost horizontal elements symbolizing the inscribed board over Christ's head, their slanted bottom elements representing his footrest. One child's monument hearkens back to Victorian times, featuring the image of a child kneeling in prayer in the company of lambs. A few monuments leave little to chance, the tombstone of one fifty-one-year-old

combining renderings of an open Bible, Easter lilies, a church window, a rising sun, and a Latin cross, all on a single stone.

The cemetery's non-religious images are equally interesting. Markers on the graves of young children often incorporate images of teddy bears or lambs, the latter image continuing to symbolize youth and innocence, just as it did a century ago. There are occasional vestiges of the old fraternal symbols so common in the community's older cemeteries: the Masonic scribe and square, the five-pointed star of the Order of the Eastern Star, and the three chain links of the Odd Fellows Lodge. More common, however, are symbols that relate to nature, occupations, recreation and sports, and, occasionally, ethnic origins. Stock images of wild roses, poppies, and maple leaves abound. There are occasional dogwood blooms, the provincial floral emblem. Scenes of the province's natural splendour abound, whether rendered in stone or bronze. There is a touching image of a married couple, reunited in death, walking across a field toward the rising sun, a symbol of eternal life. Another design features a broken split rail fence, suggestive of an earthly existence ended, but with the promise of eternal life in the mountains beyond. One commonly repeated image features tall trees flanking an opening in the forest, with rugged mountains far off in the distance. For many British Columbians, the place where they planned to spend eternity was little different from the earthly paradise they had enjoyed in life.

Others buried in the cemetery appear to have wanted to spend their afterlife continuing to do what they most enjoyed doing while alive. A sixty-nine-year-old grandmother is remembered for her love of sewing and knitting, a needle, thread, spool, and ball of yarn being prominent on her headstone. One man, who died in his mid-sixties, is remembered for his love of card games, the image of a royal flush, in spades, no less – perhaps symbolizing continued good luck in the great hereafter – embellishing his monument. For one

in his sixties is remembered for his love of steam locomotives, while an empty pickup truck parked beside a lake in the wilderness is every bit as evocative as an image of an empty chair. The grave of one fourteen-year-old boy is distinguished by images of his favourite sport: a baseball mitt, a bat, and a ball. The family of one thirteen-year-old boy harnessed a variety of symbols to preserve his memory; images of lacrosse sticks, a praying child, and a lamb adorn his memorial. Renderings of horses are also frequently encountered, especially on the graves of teenaged girls. The grave of one twenty-four-year-old woman is particularly poignant. Knowing she was seriously ill, she dreamt of swimming with dolphins. A rendering of the aquatic mammal is therefore engraved on her memorial.

Finally, there are monuments whose designs reflect ethnicity. A pair of thistles adorns the stone of a Scot who died at the age of 85. A couple, both apparently born in the Netherlands, are remembered with a cast bronze windmill, while Eastern crosses proliferate on the graves of families who trace their origins to the Ukraine. Images of Canada also abound. Clusters of maple leaves fill the corners of numerous bronze memorials, perhaps suggesting our commonalities, both as Canadians and as beings subject to mortality, each entitled to a frail memorial of our own.

seventy-four-year-old farmer, sitting on his tractor seems to have been a particular love, and an image of his tractor was thus rendered in relief on his cast bronze headstone. For two young boys, not yet licensed to drive, the hope of owning and driving a Corvette sports car was preserved in stone as an unrequited dream. Others had visions of different automobiles, an illustration of a Volkswagen Beetle being placed on the headstone of one nine-year-old boy. For the grave of a twenty-five-year-old man, the image of a single motor vehicle was not deemed sufficient, his family remembering his love of both sports coupes and motorcycles on his etched stone monument. Other young people are remembered for their interest in music, electric guitars being featured on their headstones.

Images of sports are no less common. A snowboarder flies down a mountain slope, the bracing alpine air forever blowing on his face, recalling the earthly passion of a sixteen-year-old boy. A man

REST IN PEACE

Township of
Langley

Est. 1873

Langley's Cemeteries Today

LANGLEY'S long and colourful history is reflected in its cemetery monuments. The community's cemeteries reflect over a century and a half of changing approaches to burial and memorialization. Although no tangible evidence remains, there are strong traditions of First Nations tree burials in the community. There are modest monuments dating from the time when the Hudson's Bay Company reigned supreme. The community's two oldest municipal graveyards are filled with remarkable sculptures in stone, their landscapes illustrating how the picturesque rural cemeteries established in Fort Langley and Murrayville evolved to embrace new trends in cemetery design: the lawn-park cemetery and the more recent lawn cemetery movement. The municipality's most recent cemetery, the Langley Lawn Cemetery, shows how the aesthetic and spiritual characteristics of cemeteries waned in the mid-twentieth century, but also how individuality and imagination began to re-emerge as the century drew to a close.

Today, four of Langley's burial sites – the McQuilken burial, the former Patricia Lutheran Churchyard, the 8th Avenue burials, and the 200th Street burial – remain on private property. Three or four sit on land owned by the Greater Vancouver Regional District. Two continue to be owned by the Anglican Diocese of New Westminster. The remaining three – the Fort Langley, Murrayville, and Langley Lawn cemeteries – are owned and operated by the Township of Langley. Of all of these cemeteries, only the Township's are active burial grounds. The Township's Legislative and Administrative Services staff and the Parks and Recreation Division administer Langley's three municipal cemeteries, the former attending to matters of policy and the latter providing day-to-day burial and maintenance services.

In earlier years, revenues received from the sale of cemetery plots were often used to pay the costs of daily operations. This was true of both publicly and privately owned cemeteries, in Europe as well as in North America. The arrangement worked well as long as there were lots to sell. Privately run cemeteries thus made their greatest profits in their early and middle years of operation. But when they neared capacity, their revenue streams dried up, and many went into bankruptcy or were simply closed.

In light of experiences in a number of jurisdictions, ensuring that municipalities will always have the means to maintain their cemeteries has long concerned the province. The development of perpetual care funds is now required by the provincial government. The Township's Legislative and Administrative Services staff administer the Township's perpetual care fund. A portion of

91

the fees levied for the sale of plots, for opening and closing graves, and for placing of monuments is now directed to the fund, the interest on which is intended for perpetual care purposes. Amendments made to the Cemetery Bylaw in 1997 set such fees at approximately 25 percent of the overall fee for the services mentioned.

The current bylaw sets out the full range of terms and conditions under which the Township's cemeteries are administered. Township Council is defined as the cemeteries' board of trustees. Contrary to popular belief, plots are not actually sold. Rather, licences are granted for their use, in perpetuity. An individual may "purchase" only two plots at one time, an arrangement that permits a side-by-side burial, generally of a married couple. This is a departure from earlier years, when it was common for an individual to purchase a number of plots for the use of their family. This

Langley Lawn Cemetery Columbarium

practice in some cases resulted in plots sitting empty a century after their sale. The bylaw now permits the Township to reclaim unused plots under conditions that respect the interests of the original licence holder.

The bylaw also permits up to two burials in a single grave, provided that the top of the uppermost casket is at the prescribed distance below the level of the ground. Up to eight cremated remains may also be buried in a single grave. Alternatively, cremains may be scattered in a "memory garden."

Like earlier regulations, the bylaw limits new monuments to flat, flush-mounted bronze and granite plaques. It is the Township's responsibility to encase such monuments in concrete and to place them in the cemetery. Side-by-side adult graves may be marked by larger monuments than those allowed on single graves, and markers on adult graves may be larger than those permitted on infants' graves.

All burials in Langley are also governed by the terms of the provincial Cemetery and Funeral Services Act. The provisions of the act are designed to safeguard the public interest, including the interests of deceased individuals, their families, and the community at large. Further, the act requires the appointment of a provincial registrar to administer and enforce its terms. These relate to burials, exhumations, physical maintenance, the licensing of funeral providers, funeral services, and the maintenance of records.

Today, Langley's cemeteries are places for the living as well as the dead. This becomes abundantly clear on significant occasions such as birthdays, wedding anniversaries, Mother's Day, Father's Day, Christmas, and, in the case of deceased veterans, Remembrance Day. Floral offerings, balloons, cards, and lit lanterns are often left on individual graves on such occasions, and children's graves are often decorated with stuffed animals and toys, symbols of the living reaching out to the dead.

Charnel house
A building in which bones are deposited.

Columbarium
A building in which cremated remains are deposited in sealed compartments.

Cremains
Cremated remains, ashes.

Crocket
An ornament in the form of curved or bent foliage.

Cruciform
In the form of a cross.

Cusp
Projecting points found at the meeting of foils in Gothic architecture.

Foil
A lobe or leaf-shaped curve in Gothic architecture, formed by the cusping of a circle.

Garden-park
A synonym for **landscape-lawn**.

Headboard
A tablet-form monument made of wood.

Incised
A form of sculpture in which the design is formed by cutting into a flat piece of stone, leaving the surrounding stone intact.

Inhumation
Burial underground.

Landscape-lawn
A form of cemetery design popular from the mid-nineteenth century, characterized by large expanses of lawn broken up by stands of trees, and with family, rather than individual monuments.

Lawn cemetery
A form of cemetery design popular in North America from the 1920s, characterized by flush-mounted monuments set into large, generally unbroken expanses of lawn.

Lawn-park
A synonym for **landscape-lawn**.

Ledger
A low, rectangular stone or piece of cast concrete covering a grave.

Mausoleum
An aboveground structure in which human remains are deposited, generally in sealed compartments.

Memorial garden
A garden in which cremated remains are scattered, usually without individual memorial plaques.

Memorial park
A synonym for **lawn cemetery**.

Obelisk
An upright four-sided pillar that tapers upward and terminates in a pyramid.

Pedestal
The base of a column, a plinth on which something may be placed. Early-twentieth-century tombstones often resembled pedestals, but seldom had flat tops.

Pediment
A triangular structure used as decoration in classical architecture.

Perpetual care
A system through which funds are set aside at the time plots are purchased, the interest on the funds being used for maintenance purposes, in supposed perpetuity.

Portico
A colonnade joined by an entablature or cornice at the top.

Quatrefoil
An architectural element formed from four foils. See **foil**.

Raised lead lettering
A lettering system used on early twentieth-century tombstones, where lead letters were affixed to stones in lieu of carved inscriptions.

Raised relief
A type of sculpture in which forms are left in place while the surrounding stone is cut away.

Scattering garden
A synonym for **memorial garden**.

Tablet
A vertical, flat tombstone resembling the stone tablets Moses is said to have brought down from Sinai. The Township of Langley uses this term in its bylaws in lieu of the word "plaque."

Trefoil
An ornament in the shape of a three-part leaf. See **foil**.

Adams, John, ed. *Heritage Cemeteries in British Columbia: Collected Papers*. Victoria: Victoria Branch, British Columbia Historical Federation, 1985.

———. *Historic Guide to Ross Bay Cemetery*. Victoria: Heritage Architectural Guides, 1983.

Alder Grove Heritage Society. *The Place Between: 1860–1939*, Aldergrove, B.C.: Aldergrove Heritage Society, 1993.

Allard, Jason, Papers. MSS 155. Langley Centennial Museum.

American Life Foundation and Study Institute. *American Life Collectors Annual*. Vol. 10, 1970. Watkins Glen, N.Y.: Century House, 1970.

British Columbia, Province of. *Cemetery and Funeral Services Act*. Victoria, 1996.

British Columbia and Yukon Directory. Vancouver: Sun Directories Ltd., 1934–45.

Canada. Census of Canada. 1881, 1891, and 1901.

Carlson, Keith Thor, ed. *A Stó:lō Coast Salish Historical Atlas*. Vancouver: Douglas & McIntyre, 2001.

Curl, James Stevens. *The Victorian Celebration of Death*. Detroit: Partridge Press, 1972.

Duff, Wilson. *The Upper Stalo Indians of the Fraser River of B.C.* Anthropology in British Columbia, Memoir no. 1. Victoria: British Columbia Provincial Museum, 1952.

F. G. Architectural and Planning Consultants. *Langley's Heritage: A Listing of Heritage Resources in Langley*. Langley: Corporation of the Township of Langley, 1995.

Filey, Mike. *Mount Pleasant Cemetery: An Illustrated Guide*. Toronto: Firefly Books, 1990.

Gay, John. *Highgate Cemetery: Victorian Valhalla*. London: John Murray Ltd., 1984.

Greater Vancouver Regional District Parks Department. *Derby Reach Cultural Heritage Overview*. Burnaby: GVRD Parks Department, 1996.

Gunderson, Harald. *Funeral Services in British Columbia*. Victoria: British Columbia Funeral Association, 1992.

Harris, R. Cole. *The Resettlement of British Columbia: Essays on Colonialism and Geographical Change*. Vancouver: UBC Press, 1997.

Jalland, Pat. *Death in the Victorian Family*. Oxford: Oxford University Press, 1996.

Johnson, Wellwood R. *Legend of Langley: An Account of the Early History of Fort Langley and an Intimate Story of the Lives of Some, But Not All, of the Early Pioneers of the District of Langley*. Langley: Langley Centennial Committee, 1958.

Langley, Corporation of the Township of. Cemetery bylaws, 1898, 1904, 1928, 1966, and 1994.

———. Cemetery registers, 1996.

———. Minutes of the meetings of Langley Township Council, 1873–1927. Langley Centennial Museum.

———. Township of Langley Cemeteries Collection. MSS 11. Langley Centennial Museum.

Langley Advance. 1933–75.

Maclachlan, Morag, ed. *The Fort Langley Journals, 1827–30*. Vancouver: UBC Press, 1998.

May, Trevor. *The Victorian Undertaker*. Haverfordwest: Shire Publications, 2003.

Morley, John. *Death, Heaven, and the Victorians*. London: Studio Vista, 1971.

Pearson, John. *Land of the Peace Arch*. Cloverdale, B.C.: Surrey Centennial Committee, 1958.

Philpot, Mary. "In This Neglected Spot: The Rural Cemetery Landscape in Southern British Columbia." MA thesis, University of British Columbia, 1976.

Rogak, Lisa. *Stones and Bones of New England*. Guildford, Conn.: Globe Pequot Press, 2004.

Sharon United Church. *1990 and Counting: A History of Sharon United Church, Murrayville, B.C.* Cloverdale, B.C.: Sharon United Church, 1989.

Sloane, David. *The Last Great Necessity: Cemeteries in American History*. Baltimore and London: Johns Hopkins University Press, 1991.

Sommer, Warren. *From Prairie to City: A History of the City of Langley*. Langley: City of Langley, 1999.

Sommer, Warren, and Kurt Alberts. *Langley 125: A Celebration*. Langley: Birthplace of B.C. Gallery, 1998.

Waite, Don. *The Langley Story Illustrated*. Maple Ridge, B.C.: Don Waite Publishing, 1977.

Walworth Cemetery, Papers. MSS 101. Langley Centennial Museum.

Williams British Columbia Directory. Victoria: R. T. Williams Publishing Co., 1882/83-1917.

Wrigley's British Columbia Directory. Vancouver: Wrigley Directories Ltd., 1918–32.

British Columbian: page 22

Ron Bryson: page 39, 42 upper, 48 upper, 49 lower,
    64, 68 upper, 73 lower, 92

Brian Croft: cover (*Walworth Cemetery – 1888*,
    acrylic, 2005), page 36 (*Pioneer Cemetery,
    Fort Langley*, watercolour, 2003)

Langley Advance: page 23 left, 24 right, 25

Langley Centennial Museum: page 6, 7 right,
    8, 21 right, 63

William L. Marr: page 37

Jean Monahan May: page 71

Mortimer's Monumental Works: page 18

Robert Puls: page 35

Simon Fraser University Art Gallery:
    page 5 (oil painting by John Innes, mid-1920s)

Gordon Spears: page 26

University of British Columbia Library,
    Special Collections Division: page 3 (*Fort Langley,
    Left Bank of Fraser River, Langley Buttes in Distance*,
    watercolour painting by James Alden, 1858)

All others by or from the collection of the author

The Cemeteries of Langley

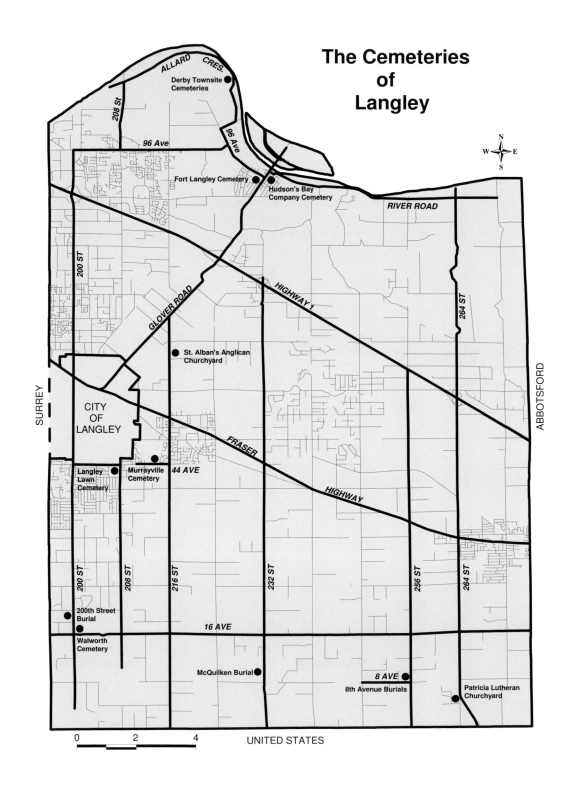

Frail Memorials: The Cemeteries of Langley